Beautiful Gardens
Round the World

THE HOUSE & GARDEN BOOK OF

Beautiful Gardens Round the World

PETER COATS

LITTLE, BROWN AND COMPANY
BOSTON   TORONTO

Frontispiece A zodiacal dial framed by the flowers of bougainvillea, on the wall of the terrace at the Ivanovic villa overlooking the bay of Formentor in Majorca.

Library of Congress Catalog Card no. 85–80128

First American edition

First published in Great Britain in 1985 by George Weidenfeld & Nicolson Ltd 91 Clapham High Street, London SW4 7TA

Printed and bound in Italy

CONTENTS

FOREWORD

Robin Herbert

President of the Royal Horticultural Society

I am delighted to have been invited to write a Foreword to this book which brings together in one volume many of the most beautiful gardens round the world.

Interest in how others have faced the challenges of creating a garden has never been greater, and gardening today is, in every sense, a growth industry. For those gardeners who seek inspiration for themselves there is much to be found in this book. It provides an opportunity to admire those elements of human genius that have created, in a variety of different cultures, and over many hundreds of years, so many idyllic settings.

International Garden Festivals in recent years have focussed our attention on the way in which gardening has developed and is carried on in different countries of the world. This book expands that theme and highlights the many different ways in which beautiful gardens have been created in response to different geographic and cultural influences.

In addition to the sheer pleasure of reading such a book, there is ample opportunity for all with an interest in gardening to add to their knowledge of how different plants and features can be brought together for best effect.

Peter Coats is ideally qualified by experience and professional expertise as a gardener and a writer to have made such a difficult selection of gardens. His photographs and helpful descriptions together succeed in creating an atmosphere whereby the reader can envisage not only the beauty but also imagine the sounds and smells. Whatever their existing knowledge of gardens, all who pick up this book will surely be entranced.

Opposite Rhododendrons grown under ideal conditions in acid soil and under light shade give of their best in early summer. These were photographed in the garden, near the Welsh border, of Lydney Park in Gloucestershire, home of Lord and Lady Bledisloe.

INTRODUCTION

Voltaire, in a more human moment than he often enjoyed, once advised fathers of families to instil a love of gardens into their children. 'It will do them good.'

It is said that the earliest gardeners in history were three beautiful girls whose father was Hesperus, the Evening Star. They had a garden in Morocco, where all the fruit was of gold, and in the care of a watchful dragon that never slept. I owe that interesting piece of garden-lore to my old friend Harold Nicolson, who, with his famous wife Vita, created what is probably the most beautiful garden in England, at Sissinghurst in Kent, which is visited, with no danger from dragons, by tens of thousands of visitors every year, a golden legacy.

But what about the Garden of Eden? That would certainly seem to be the very first garden of all – and laid out by God himself. We know that Adam was a gardener (Shakespeare, Tennyson and Kipling all describe him as such) but we do not hear of Eve pruning, and we know both picked leaves: but that was for sartorial reasons. Two witty characters in Oscar Wilde's *A Woman of No Importance* describe the Bible as a book which begins with a man and a woman in a garden, and ends with Revelations.

This book, on an infinitely humbler level, deals entirely with gardens, some very famous, some less well known: I hope that my pictures (for most of the pictures are mine) and the text will reveal something of the beauty and fascination of these gardens from all over the world – from Japan to California, and South Africa, via Mauritius, to India. As I took the majority of the pictures, I, of course, visited most of the gardens, spending happy days, among the flowers, on the springing turf and between the fountains.

In the last years of the Second World War, I was Comptroller to the penultimate Viceroy of India, Lord Wavell. One of my duties was to supervise the Viceregal gardens in Delhi.

After the war, soon after I was demobilized, I was asked by friends to advise them on the rehabilitation of their garden; the house had done wartime duty as a hospital, and the grounds had fallen into neglect.

The garden had been laid out in a series of 'rooms', each planted in a different colour scheme. This technique I developed, and as my plant vocabulary grew, I was able to carry out my schemes more and more effectively. I was lucky enough to have the help of three expert gardeners, an almost unheard-of luxury today, when owners of quite large gardens have to make do often with almost no help at all.

As the reputation of the garden grew, I suppose mine as a gardener must have grown too, I was asked to join *House & Garden* and have been with the magazine as Garden Editor for many years. In that capacity I have been lucky enough to visit some of the finest and most beautiful gardens in this country and all over the world. I went to see them with a view to subsequently describing them in the pages of the magazine and in doing so I

Opposite Ireland has some of the most beautiful gardens, thanks in some part to the mild climate and regular soft Irish rain. One of the finest is at Birr Castle, Co. Offaly, home of the Earl and Countess of Rosse. In the picture, a foliage-festooned pergola of baroque shape, devised by Anne, Lady Rosse, a sister of the stage designer Oliver Messel, leads to a garden of rhododendrons.

Above left France is famous for its formal parterres of box hedges, like this elaborate layout, at the Château de Hauteville in Dordogne. *Above right* Wales boasts several famous gardens such as Powis Castle, Duffryn, and, of course, the prestigious Bodnant. Here, at the Dower House of Bodnant, a sphinx regards, unmoved, a threatening sky. *Below right* In Washington D.C., white wisteria drapes a wall in the Dumbarton Oaks' garden, famed for its beauty.

learnt much about plants and gardens, and about gardeners.

In this book, I have chosen wherever possible to show gardens that are typical of the countries in which they are situated. It has not always been possible. We all have a strong idea of what a French garden looks like: symmetrical parterres of flowers, lines of trees, all exactly the same shape and, if it is a very large garden – Versailles for instance, or Vaux le Vicomte – perhaps a canal and certainly statues, 'staring stonily into space'. French gardens are famous, very beautiful, but somehow a little overpowering. One could hardly play cricket with the children in the garden at Versailles, or have a cup of tea in the shade.

Spanish gardens, too, evoke a definite picture. Courtyards; the Spanish word *patio* is known, and used the world over. Fountains, certainly, and the most vibrant of geraniums. Italian gardens are rather the same, though someone has usually forgotten to water the flowers. But there, too, there are statues and more fountains, and balustrades and steps. And all would be beautified, as are the Spanish gardens of Raixa and Alfabia (see pages

Above Holland has inspired gardens everywhere, usually of tulips. This one is in Kensington Gardens. London. *Right* In Japan gardens are made of raked sand, water and carefully placed rocks, as here, where they are used as stepping stones.

102–3), by the priceless patina of age. Real Spanish gardens are usually two or three hundred years old.

Japanese gardens present their own very definite image. Raked sand, thoughtfully placed rocks, bonsais – another word internationally recognized – and stone lanterns.

But what about Belgium, or Australia, or Denmark, or even the great USA? No typical garden comes to mind when one thinks of those countries, though I described in my *Great Gardens of the Western World* a special sort of garden, which could only be found in America, but in only one part of that vast country where, alone in the gardening world, the right extraordinary physical conditions exist. The gardens I mean, of course, are the gardens on the James River in South Carolina, of which I once wrote, and of one in particular, the transcendentally beautiful Magnolia Gardens, 'In the Baedeker guide for America in 1900 there are only three sights which were considered worthy of two stars. The Niagara Falls, the Grand Canyon and Magnolia Gardens'.

The longest chapter of the book is devoted to British gardens, for this is a British book: and the British are, they say, a nation of gardeners. England, Scotland, Wales and Northern Ireland must surely have the greatest variety of gardens of any country in the world.

Gardens have, since the dawn of time, been the theme of poets. For Thomas Brown a garden was (ugh!) a lovesome thing, for Kipling the whole of England was a garden, Marvell boasted that his garden was, with roses and lilies, 'quite overgrown'. Isaiah wrote of 'a garden of cucumbers' and Solomon urged his beloved to come into his garden and share his fruit.

In that great book – Voltaire again – Candide, after all his adventures, only wanted to cultivate his garden. He could have done much worse.

Above South Africa has a unique flora all its own and its native flowers such as geraniums, Arum lilies and blue agapanthus, or African lilies, have emigrated all over the world.
Left Georgia, USA: Summer houses have always found a place in gardens, as this one in Atlanta, designed by the distinguished architect, Philip Schutze.
Opposite In England, no garden would be considered complete without roses, as in the Hampshire garden at Hurst Mill of Mr and Mrs Peter Simon.

UNITED STATES

A vast country of many different climates and gardens

How can one write a general introduction to a fourteen page chapter on American gardens? The United States is not one country but twenty, with twenty different climates. There is no such thing as a typical American garden.

But perhaps I am wrong. Perhaps the typical American garden has a white picket fence, neat beds of much loved flowers such as Morning Glories and Black–Eyed Susans. And yet – did I hear the faint cry of the Mocking Bird mocking me? As I remember the pink and white fairyland of Virginia in dogwood time: I smell woodsmoke, and remember the blaze of autumn colour of the woods along the Hudson. Above all, I recall the gardens, not typical of America, but unique to America, for nowhere else in the world will you find them, the gardens along the James River in South Carolina: gardens which owe their very special romance and atmosphere to the very special setting in which they grow: a setting of towering Swamp Cypresses, rising like 'the columns of a cathedral nave' from water dyed inky black by their roots. Above are the branches of oaks hung with veils of Spanish moss (*Tillandsia usneioides*), and all mirrored in the water beneath. Two gardens in particular I remember, and always will, Cypress and Magnolia.

Left and right Graceful bridges enhance flower colour and tree trunk reflections at Magnolia gardens near Charleston.

A unique garden of topiary in Maryland – a great gardener's legacy

The Ladew Gardens near Monkton in Maryland are among the finest and most curious gardens in America. First planted in 1929, they have grown to their present state of development and beauty over the last fifty years. They are curious because the art of topiary has never been so popular in America as it is in Europe.

The word topiary derives from the Greek *topos*, a place, and so *topiarius* came to mean 'the man in charge of the place', hence gardener. Topiary was known to the Romans, and Pliny the Younger describes hedges of clipped box in his Tuscan villa. But nowhere was it more popular than in England, and perhaps it was when Ladew was fox-hunting in Leicestershire, which he did for many years running, that he was inspired by the clipped cones, goblets, peacocks and spirals which he must have seen in old English gardens.

Today the glory of the Ladew gardens is the art of topiary – the craft of trimming box, bay, phillyrea or yew. Harvey Ladew planted miles of hedges of quick-growing Japanese yew (*Taxus cuspidata*) and devised for them some special features not usually seen carved out of evergreens.

Swans were a favourite motif – and even a pack of hounds, racing across a lawn in full cry after a fox; all in meticulously sculpted box.

Opposite top left A pillar of the covered arcade frames an inner courtyard with a sun-welcoming bow window and white clapboard wall. The planting is of white candytuft with yellow iris. *Top centre* One of the many perfectly trimmed hedges has windows cut in it, and a decorative, crisply painted garden gate. *Top right* A swan in greenery breasts a wave of lilac blossom. *Left* Massed tulips lay a carpet of colour under a topiary yew carved in the shape of a lyre bird. *Above* Elaborate swagged topiary. To left and right, putti with pipes and taborin sound a welcome. *Below* The 'Berry Garden' designed as a 'fall and winter feast for birds'. The central planting is of *Pachysandra terminalis*, cotoneaster and yew, with hollies, crab apples, hawthorn and skimmia beyond.

Harvey Ladew, like many experienced and artistic gardeners, did not consider that a garden was complete without water, so he conjured a handsome fountain in the centre of the main lawn of his garden. He also had to have a rose garden like the ones he had admired in England, planted with varieties which are well loved in America. Many indeed were raised in the United States, roses such as the pink, constant flowerer 'Aloha', the vividly cinnamon 'Chrysler Imperial' and the lovely 'Golden Showers'.

The house itself, which is approached by a graceful covered arcade, is about a hundred and fifty years' old.

When embarking on the planting of his extraordinary but fascinating garden Ladew is quoted as having said, 'I decided to do all the designing myself – and I made mistakes, but it was I who made them, and I learned from them.'

Forty odd years later, in 1971, Ladew was awarded the Distinguished Service Medal of the Garden Club of America for creating this outstanding topiary garden in America, without professional aid.

Besides being an inspired garden maker, and a keen fox-hunting man, Ladew was a wit: on a sundial in his garden, instead of the usual inscription 'Tempus fugit', he had engraved Hilaire Belloc's words 'I am a sundial, and I make a botch, Of what is done far better by a watch.'

Above Between pyramids of sharply tailored yew the plume of a central fountain blows in the Maryland breeze.
Left A graceful covered arcade leads from the main house, which was built about 1830, to a conically roofed summer house.

The garden at Dumbarton Oaks, outside Washington, a pleasure-ground of international renown and style

When the property of Dumbarton Oaks was bought by Mr and Mrs Robert Bliss in 1920, it consisted of a rundown house set in uncared-for grounds. But there were compensations. The site looked over beautiful views towards the Rock Creek ravine, and there were good trees, which have been carefully preserved. The garden, which is surely one of the most famous in the world, was designed by the brilliant Beatrix Farrand, and her first care was to make 'the plan fit the ground' and not twist the ground to fit the plan. It should also be mentioned that it was at Dumbarton Oaks

that the original international meeting took place in 1944, in the dark days of the war, which led to the creation of the United Nations. There can be no other garden in the world which can lay claim to such renown.

Mrs Bliss had always dreamed of creating a great garden. Her husband had seen diplomatic service in many foreign countries, and with the help of the talented Beatrix Farrand, Mrs Bliss collated the ideas she had gathered on her travels to plan and plant her unique pleasureground.

It is a garden with whispers of Italy in its

Above The formal rose garden where the massive shapes of English box act as foils for the delicate early foliage of the rose bushes.

carved stone balustrades, soaring flights of steps, and in the splash of fountains. There are touches of France in its terraces and occasional formality. And, here and there, there are corners which might be in England, with parts of the garden designed very much in the style still popular in England today – though introduced over eighty years ago by an American, Laurence Johnston at the garden he made famous, at Hidcote in Gloucestershire. Namely, the outdoor stone or hedge-walled rooms, with the sky for ceiling, sheltered corners for sitting out and, who knows, for world-shaping conversation? On the walls of one wisteria-hung enclosure there hangs a plaque with a quotation (in Italian) from Dante's *Divine Comedy* which is a fitting tribute to this great American creation. Translated it runs 'Those who in ancient times have famed in song the Age of Gold … dreamed of this place, upon Parnassus.'

Top left The careful architecture of the garden is curtained and enhanced, but not smothered, by flowers and foliage. *Below left* The fine features of a decorative stone fountain give the garden an air of Italy. *Opposite top left* The Star, the smallest and one of the most charming of the 'garden rooms'. Paved in the design of a giant star in lead and stone, it is hedged with white azaleas. *Top right* An impeccably designed pergola offers shade on sunny days. *Below* The pebble garden with its swirling baroque pattern is kept permanently wet with a shallow layer of water, a popular place for birds to splash about in. It was at one time a tennis court.

Fantastic Viscaya, a Renaissance garden reborn in Florida

The Villa Viscaya, and its extraordinary gardens, were conjured over seventy years ago on the coral, or rather key-stone, strand of Biscayne Bay, Florida, by the imagination – and fortune – of James Deering, of the Deering Harvester Company. F. Burrall Hoffman (born 1884) was the architect of the Villa itself and the Colombian Diego Suarez (1888–1974) of the gardens, which are surely some of the most spectacular in the United States, if not the world. Their total success is due not only to the flair and verve of the architect, but also, in part, to the curious consistency of the local key-stone – a form of coral, veined and furrowed in a unique way, which quickly takes on an ancient-seeming, lichen-grown patina. The balustrades, grottoes, pillars and stair-flights of Viscaya look as if they have been there since the Renaissance, rather than only since 1914.

Recently, the gardens have been restored to great beauty. The many architectural features are set off by boldly coloured well-maintained parterres, while waterlilies star the many pools. All around are the differing outlines of tamarinds and oaks, hung with the ropy arms of vines.

Opposite above Richly carved urns, baskets of fruit and capitals, with the façade of Viscaya beyond. *Below left* The east sea front, overlooking Biscayne Bay. *Below centre* Steps from the 'Casino' down to the water, recall a small canal in Venice. *Below right* A stone barge breakwater. *Above* Obelisks reflected in water. All around the garden are remnants of the South Florida Hammock Forest. *Below* An interior courtyard set with pillars and palm trees.

Top row, *left* Sculptured giants play portals to a shaded grotto. *Right* A parterre of begonias and mop-headed trees. *Second row*, *left* As box does not thrive in the climate of Florida, many hedges are of pine and a native jasmine. *Right* The stone soon takes on an ancient-seeming and lichenous patina. *Third row*, *left* A Roman sarcophagus near the main entrance. *Centre* A pillar of clipped foliage framed in a leafy arch. *Right* A garden door set in rusticated stone. *Bottom row*, *left* Waterlilies in a pillared pool. *Right* The 'Casino'. *Opposite* An elaborate but meticulously kept *broderie* in evergreen.

Spring in Virginia – the garden at Agecroft Hall

How many plants Britain owes to America. One wonders what English parks could have looked like without, say, wellingtonia (in America, washingtonia) or taxodium or robinia, to name but three; our shrubberies without *Mahonia aquifolium*, *Magnolia grandiflora* or any of the ceanothus; or our borders without lobelia, *Phlox drummondii*, and the countless other plants we have long ceased to think of as American importations.

But if we owe much to the Americans, the British influence in the design and overall appearance of gardens in America has been strong, and one of the loveliest gardens in Virginia has a very English look – Agecroft Hall.

The house itself has had, literally, a *mouvementé* history. It was built in England in the late 1400s for the Langley family of Lancashire. For nearly 500 years it was a much-loved, lived-in home. Then, in 1925, with the industrialization of the part of Lancashire in which it was situated, the house fell on bad times and, at one point was due for demolition. Then fortune smiled. Richmonders 'of distinction and appreciation', lovers of England and traditional English architecture, Mr and Mrs Thomas Williams, bought the threatened building. The old house was carefully taken down, each stone and beam was numbered, and the whole shipped across the Atlantic, where it was lovingly recreated in its present beautiful setting.

Above Pink and white planting and a formal plan. *Below* A simply designed path, overhung with a tracery of branches, set on either side with white azaleas. *Opposite above* The sunk Box Garden was inspired by the one at Hampton Court, near London. *Below left* A classical urn set in greenery and flower-bordered paths of tiles. *Below right* Steps, and more azaleas. Above is the tree which is the glory of Virginia in the spring – the famous dogwood (*Cornus florida*) which, to many a British gardener's regret, does not thrive in England, as winters are not cold enough, and summers too cool.

CANADA

The Butchart gardens flourish in the gentle temperature of Vancouver

Canada is not a country that one associates with luxuriant, and certainly not with exotic vegetation. Maples certainly, and the maple leaf has become the Canadian national emblem. But acers grow all over the world, and change colour in autumn as spectacularly in the suburbs of Tunbridge Wells or Tokyo as they do in Toronto.

Miss Isabella Preston raised beautiful and perfectly hardy lilacs in the rigorous climate of Canada at Ottawa in 1920: and there are few more beautiful lilacs than some of the Preston hybrids, and for once they have beautiful names to match: 'Bellicent', 'Hiawatha' and, of course, 'Isabella'. By this, I do not mean that they are better lilacs than those raised by the great Lemoine, but they are certainly beautiful, and different for they have attractive foliage, the European lilacs' inherent weakness. There are few trees duller with their drab green leaves, when not in flower, than the popular 'Souvenir de Louis Spaeth' or the much acclaimed 'Masséna'. But, say the connoisseurs, what about *Cornus canadensis*? Well, what about it? A pretty enough ground-coverer, which needs an acid soil, and has small four-petalled flowers. But Thomas Nuttall (1786–1859) discovered one of the best of all cornus (it bears, quite rightly, his name) near Vancouver, and the great Douglas fir was collected in Canada, as well as the almost too popular *Mahonia aquifolium* by that ill-fated Scot, David Douglas. Diervilla, gaultheria and the beautiful trillium originated in Canada, and from there have been scattered all over the world; the Douglas fir, in particular, not only to grace private parks and gardens, but to do sterling, if unromantic, work in afforestation schemes.

It was on the West Coast of Canada that I saw – for its fame had reached me – one of the great gardens of the world, the Butchart gardens at Victoria, in British Columbia, a garden ennobled by its unique site, lavish planting and brightened with the vigour of youth, for it is only sixty years old.

The history of the Butchart garden is short, but interesting, and can be quickly told. The Butchart family, attractive, intelligent and successful, made their fortune in cement. They were also inventive; for instance, they were the first cement firm to think of delivering their product in easily handled sacks, instead of cumbrous barrels.

Robert Pym Butchart, the firm's founder, discovered that there were rich deposits of limestone on the Saanich peninsula, some miles to the north of Victoria. He established a cement plant there, early in this century. The opening of the plant coincided with a building boom all over Canada and the United States, so the Butchart firm prospered, and the Butchart family found Tod Inlet, near where the valuable deposits lay, an attractive area in itself. They built a handsome house there, and settled down.

About twenty years later the limestone quarrying activities moved on, leaving an unsightly chasm. Mrs Butchart, not only beautiful, but imaginative and adventurous (she once flew with Louis Blériot

Above In one of the many enclosed gardens, a glassy pond studded with waterlily pads is surrounded with a riotous planting of begonias. *Opposite* Much thought has been given to the colour schemes in this Canadian Eden. What was once a quarry has been transformed into a happy blend of flower and leaf colour. In the foreground, the silver of *Cineraria maritima*, with pink asters and red pelargoniums beyond. In the distance the delicate gold of trees foretells the autumn.

(1872–1936), first man to fly the English Channel), had the idea of making the chasm, and its surroundings, into a garden. With little knowledge, but a great deal of enthusiasm, Jenny Butchart set to work. The cliff-like rock face was considered ugly. Jenny, rather hazardously, had herself let down in a bo'sun's chair, by ropes, armed with a trowel and a sack of good soil, to stuff ivies, and other creepers, into any receptive crevice. Hundreds of tons of top soil were brought by horse and cart: a lake was scooped out, and made watertight (with Butchart's cement, one assumes). Full-grown trees were transplanted, and rare plants brought from all over the world.

Throughout this Canadian Eden thought has been given to the blendings and combinations of colours. What was once a quarry has been transformed over the years into the happiest chiaroscuro of flower and leaf colour, the latter providing a fireworks-like display every fall.

Robert and Jenny Butchart have gone, but the gardens are devotedly looked after by their grandchildren, Ian and Ann Lee Ross. They are visited by tens of thousands of people every year, and certainly no one is disappointed.

Opposite above The Ross fountain, surely one of the most spectacular fountains in the world, with its weaving, interlacing jets. In the foreground, the lavender-like spires of *Salvia farinacea*. To the left, the old quarry walls. *Below left* A curiously clipped evergreen takes on the appearance of sculpture. *Below right* Entwined bronze dolphins, cast in Italy, enclose a foaming jet. *Above* Swathes of flower colour, set off by silver leaves, in the sunk garden. *Below* Branches overhang a large lily pond, with its banks planted thickly with moisture-loving hostas.

JAPAN

Gardens with a tranquil mystique of their own

The story of Japanese gardens can really be said to start in the twelfth century, at a time when in Europe and America there were, to all intents, no gardens at all. Two factors have always played important roles in Japanese garden design: space – or the lack of it – and the relationship between garden and house, a relationship that we in the western world only came to appreciate many centuries later.

Japan is a comparatively small country, and space is, therefore, valuable. Hence the almost universally modest proportions of Japanese gardens. Hence, too, the special artistic techniques and conventions evolved in order to include the various features considered essential. The Japanese garden designer is adept at the exercise of *trompe l'oeil*: the garden, rarely larger than the size of a tennis court, must seem larger than it is. It must include a lake – for tranquility and for coolness in the burning Japanese summer – so a pond, though only a few feet across is 'extended' by skilful planting, or, if water is unavailable, replaced with a stretch of raked sand. The 'lake', ideally, should be set among mountains, so these are represented by rocks, and the mystique about placing the rocks would take pages to explain. The pond-lake must curve cunningly out of sight behind the rock-mountain. The stone lantern must be half-hidden by foliage, and the house itself half-hidden by medium-sized trees such as cherries, maples or pines. Achievement of the right scale is all important.

Japan has no great rivers, like the Potomac or even the Thames. Japanese rivers rush down in swift streams and gushing cascades on their short journeys from the mountains to the sea. Therefore, in a small garden in Kyoto or Osaka, the sound of a miniature waterfall is another essential status symbol.

The relationship between garden and house is all important. It has been evolved over the centuries by the Japanese far more skilfully than by the

Left Japanese gardens are for meditation and reflections. *Opposite* Light foliage and rock-work seen through an eye-shaped window, framed in Shojis of paper.

western world so far – with sliding walls, open verandahs and paved paths which lead to the house terrace and sometimes right into the house itself. Overall, and especially in the immediate vicinity of the main building, there are corners to be turned, a leaf-hedged path curving away – to where? Some question unanswered, some mystery unexplained. But, as the famous poet Matsuo Basho wrote in the seventeenth century, 'If everything is at once expressed, what is there left?'

Moss, rocks and raked sand

Opposite above The Moss garden at Saiho-Ji in Kyoto. The boles of the trees rise out of a meticulous carpet of moss. *Below left* The placing of rocks in raked sand is a significant element, as in the famous Ryoan-Ji garden. *Below centre* A popular feature in Japanese gardens are balustrades lacquered a warm red. *Below right* In autumn the colour scheme assumes a more varied form, with red-leafed maples and golden bamboos. Here formal shapes are supplied by clipped azaleas, an art at which the Japanese excel. *Right* Informally cut stones set in moss or ground-hugging ivy, lead to a typical bridge of bamboo. Different greens play an important part in classically planned Japanese gardens: flower colour is considered less important.

Left and below Blossom canopies a flight of steps, and an informal path of stones set in gravel lead to a tea pavilion in the Imperial Katsura garden. *Opposite* A giant sculpture of a lion-dog, a kind of outsize pekinese, is often installed as sentinel to a shrine.

Features and fashions in Japanese gardening have been adopted in gardens all over the world

Opposite Bridges in the Japanese style have been copied in Europe and America. For the Japanese the bridge played not only a useful, but a decorative part in their garden scheme. As early as in the twelfth century bridges were painted a brilliant vermilion – the bright lacquer in striking contrast with the greenery all around. It was not until later that flower colour, such as that of cherry trees and azaleas, was introduced into gardens. The bridge on the left, though perhaps not ideally comfortable to cross, forms, with its reflection in the water below, a perfect circle. A typical Japanese gateway or Shiorido, which could easily be copied in Western gardens and would, at once, lend an Oriental air. The one on the right stands in a verdant setting of pine trees and clipped maples. A stone lantern is grown around with that most beautiful and useful of Japanese shrubs, *Pieris japonica*, with its evergreen foliage and bright coppery young foliage in spring (not scarlet, as is *P. forrestii*, which comes from China) and graceful panicles of cream-coloured flowers. The dim rays from such stone lanterns often lit up the important tea-drinking ceremony. This graceful garden-object was photographed thousands of miles from Japan – in the famous English garden of Nymans, in East Sussex. From Sussex to Georgia, USA. A bamboo-roofed gateway of wood and lattice work, designed in Japan, and shipped to the new botanic garden at Atlanta, where it seems to have made itself perfectly at home. Three elements of a Japanese garden come together to make a telling photograph – in Canada. Raked sand, fallen red leaves of *Acer japonica*, a red-lacquered bridge, in the Butchart garden near Victoria in Vancouver. *Right above* An elaborate lantern in lead decorated with fish finials. In the background, trees with an oriental twist. Photographed in a garden famous for its rhododendrons, Pylewell Park in Hampshire, England. *Right* Japanese bronze cranes, or Tsuru, strike graceful attitudes far from home. Photographed in the garden of the Hanbury family at La Mortola, near Ventimiglia in Italy.

AUSTRALIA

Home thoughts from abroad.
The Englishness of Australian gardens

Australia is a country not famous for its gardens. Taken as a whole, the climate is harsh and, in such a vast area, variable. Plants, introduced from other countries, unless cultivated with constant care, and under ideal conditions, which are rare, either fade away or proliferate alarmingly, as rabbits did. To mention just one – the prickly pear: a few years after its introduction it covered an area of 70,000 square miles (181,000 sq. km): the total area of England and Wales being 58,000 square miles (151,000 sq. km). Difficult to destroy by chemical or mechanical means, it needed the importation of 300,000,000 caterpillars to eradicate it – an example of Australian pertinacity and imagination. But wherever the Anglo-Saxon settles, there will be gardens, whatever the difficulties: and, sheltered by those beautiful natives of Australia, eucalyptus and mimosa, there are not only great public gardens, like the one shown on these two pages, but private gardens large and small.

Above The Waratah flower (*Telopea speciosissima*), acclaimed as the national flower of Australia. *Left* and *opposite* Lavish planting in one of Sydney's splendid parks.

Milton Park – a great garden in New South Wales

Milton Park, Bowral, the stud quarters of King Ranch (Australia) Ltd, has one of the oldest and most famous gardens in New South Wales. It was begun in 1910 when Anthony Hordern bought the 1,200-acre property.

The garden is essentially a spring garden – that is, it is at its best in the months of September, October and November, when lilacs, dogwoods, rhododendrons and azaleas are at their peak.

Once shelter was established, the good drainage and rich natural volcanic soil combined to make an ideal environment for the planting of imported species of ash, elm, maple and beech trees. The sandstone used for the walls and paths through the garden was found on the property and many of the blocks were convict-hewn.

Water plays a part in the garden architecture of Milton Park, and a waterfall and

Opposite The house, in its setting of flowers and trees. *Above* Neatly laid paving for easy walking. *Above right* Azaleas sheltered by a wall of convict-hewn stone. *Below right* Standard wisterias and bronze cranes from Japan.

pool are the latest additions to the landscaping, made by Mr and Mrs Peter Baillieu.

In 1932, the garden was replanned – it was 'opened up', hedges were removed and the long curves and sweeping vistas were created.

An English garden transported

Sir Jock and Lady Pagan's garden at Kennerton Green, in Bowral, New South Wales, as can be seen from the pictures on these two pages, might have been transported root, stalk and blossom, from some attractive village in Hampshire. Walking round it, you expect to hear blackbirds singing, but they are more likely to be kookaburras. The garden is sheltered by trees, which have quickly come to maturity. When these pictures were taken, it was November, early spring, and the young leaves were just showing the freshest green. The Pagan borders were the picture of spring, and all Lady Pagan's favourite flowers had thoughtfully put on a show for us: tree peonies, surely one of the grandest of all plants, were flowering sumptuously, iris, in all the colours of the rainbow, after which, of course, they are named. In Greek mythology, Iris was not only the personification of the rainbow, but also the messenger of the Gods. Virgil has it that she was named after the rainbow, because the rainbow was the path along which she travelled. Near the iris grew pink forget-me-nots, which once puzzled that noted Australian flower painter, Paul Jones: he is reported to have exclaimed in disbelief, 'But forget-me-nots are blue.'

Some roses were already in flower when I was at Kennerton Green – many others were in promising bud. Special favourites included 'Mount Shasta' as white as 'Virgo', growing nearby. Lady Pagan loves white roses, and sighs, 'If only one had the courage to have only "Iceberg".' As a garden designer, I rather agree with her.

For gardeners in Australia, water – or lack of it – can be a worry. Summer heat and hot winds are other hazards.

Lady Pagan admits to growing mostly English plants in her garden, but some Australian natives are favourites, too. The claret ash (*Fraxinus* 'Raywood' var.), an attractive sorbus for instance, raised in Australia, and a golden elm (*Ulmus dampieri*), among them.

The Pagans visit England regularly, and though they have a beautiful garden in Australia, after seeing Hidcote and Sissinghurst, they admit that when they get home 'We feel like ploughing our own garden up and starting again'. They would make a great mistake.

Above left An informal path, with
cushions of overhanging plants. *Above
right* Luxurious rhododendron flowers
and silver birch. *Below left* A place to
relax. *Below right* Comfortable steps invite
the visitor to refreshment. *Opposite above*
Spring foliage and trellised porch. *Below*
Spring flower and colourful groundcover.

SINGAPORE

Lush growth, brilliant colour on Singapore island

When Sir Stamford Raffles, that great colonial administrator (1781–1826), founded, in 1820, the island settlement that was to become the city of Singapore, he laid out a botanic garden soon afterwards, which certainly showed confidence in his enterprise. Today Singapore is an island composed of gardens. Many nationalities make up the city's population, two of the leading ones being the Chinese and the Japanese. Each has its own garden: the Chinese one complete with pagoda. Both these exotic pleasuregrounds lie near the tranquil waters of the Jurong lake. A third garden must not be missed, John Ede's magnificent Mandai Orchid Garden, in the north part of the island. One of its many beautiful features is a water garden. In the cool moisture of the microclimate it creates flourish the yucca-like leaves of dracaenas, while the water itself, as might be expected, is strewn with waterlilies. The decorative pool is spanned by a low wooden bridge, and all around are billowing groups of shrubs with tropical and sometimes scented foliage, so that the eyes and nostrils of the visitor are pleasantly assailed by bright colours or seductive fragrances.

Left John Ede's lily pond in his garden of many colours. *Opposite top left and centre* A palm tree displays its soaring fronds, and lily pads fill a corner of a stone-kerbed pool. The many thousands who visit the garden every year carry away memories of a water garden with banks of orchids, and multi-coloured foliage stretching 'like a brilliant carpet across two hillsides'. *Top right* Central feature of the Chinese garden is a lofty pagoda. *Centre left* A kaleidoscope of colour, the golden tones being supplied by the luxuriant leaves of crotons, and crimson by the wine-tinted foliage of iresine, one of the Amarantaceae, and a plant sometimes used in western gardens to brighten bedding-out schemes: only half-hardy, it has, of course, to be raised in a greenhouse. *Centre right* An Oriental garden with a Mediterranean look. A corner of the Chinese garden, its skyline broken by the sharp outline of cypresses. *Below left* Topiary in a tope, and for readers who do not speak Tamil, tope means 'an enclosed plantation'. Beyond, a traditional red and white wall of the Chinese garden, with a gracefully arched gateway. *Below right* A burst of lush verdure almost overgrows a slat-house in John Ede's garden.

INDIA

The garden of the Rashtrapati Bhavan, former Viceroy's house

I have chosen, of all the gardens of India, the gardens of the Rashtrapati Bhavan because, as mentioned in the Introduction, I was, to some extent, in charge of them. In my position of Comptroller my duties were many and varied, but the garden did come under my direction; though it was a comparatively minor care. Harold Nicolson has described me, somewhat imaginatively, as overseeing armies of gardeners 'resplendent in gold and white uniform, presiding over the Lutyens garden at Delhi, directing with a wave of a trowel this stupendous creation, stepping gingerly among the cannas and the golden orioles. Never since the days of Xenophon has a soldier, and an aide de camp to boot, been so precise and efficient a gardener ...' All very fine and fancy, but I did manage, by ploughing up part of the golf course, to grow tons of vegetables, much needed in the hospitals.

I have chosen what was once the Viceroy's garden for various reasons. First, it is a masterly reconstruction, by an architect of genius, Sir Edwin Lutyens, of a Mogul Garden – in fact, it was always known as the Mogul Garden and it demonstrates, though on a larger scale, the way the Moguls planned and planted their pleasuregrounds 400 years ago; unlike the few Indian gardens of that period that survive, it is perfectly maintained. The parterres of flowers still blaze, the fountains – an essential part of any Oriental garden – still throw up their glistening columns of water towards the cloudless Indian sky. The steps, terraces and colonnades remain uncrumbled and the avenues of Ashok trees, beloved of Indian garden planners through the centuries, still cast their welcome shade. In my two years of close association with this magnificent garden, I never saw a golden oriole, but there were hoopoes pecking about on the lawns and the occasional fly-past, low among the trees, of flocks of parrots which Kipling likened to 'green shrapnel'.

The garden of the Rashtrapati Bhavan was planned in the 1920s by Lutyens' master hand on the lines of a garden that the Emperor Akbar might have laid out for his palace at Fatehpur-Sikri: and it has already blossomed and grown in beauty for many years longer than that great Mogul's garden, for as every student of Indian history knows, the Emperor Akbar's elegant new capital was abandoned to the parrots and chipmunks, after a mere thirty or so years, owing to the failure of the water supply.

The garden lies behind the west front of what is now the President's palace, and is intersected by avenues of evergreen trees and sparkling canals – no shortage of water here. Three great fountains, and many smaller ones, give lightness and glitter to the scene. The three large fountains are really spectacular, and were built in the form of giant tiers of shallow saucers. The writer Robert Byron rather prosaically described them as 'red stone pennies'. Actually the design was inspired by the vast leaf pads of the

Opposite Sir Edwin Lutyens' masterly reconstruction of a Mogul garden.

Victoria regia waterlily. All around, like an Oriental carpet, lie beds of bright flowers, kept low so as not to blur the overall carefully devised design.

When time allowed, I used to stroll round the garden with the redoubtable but friendly, English garden superintendant, Mr Reader. Some beds were planted with English flowers such as verbena, petunias and gerberas: others blazed almost too brazenly with the favourite with all Indian gardeners, canna lilies. Tactfully, I sometimes made suggestions, which would soften, and make less strident the chiaroscuro. Fewer cannas perhaps, or at least fewer pillarbox red and orange ones. Surely I had seen cream coloured cannas in the Commander-in-Chief's garden? Could we not have pink or white geraniums instead of scarlet ones? Mr Reader listened indulgently, and next year the overall colour scheme was indeed kinder to the retina. *Phlox drummondii*, in half a dozen sweet pea colours, were introduced. A blue flower – with blue stems – which I had never seen before, *Salvia farinacea*, made its appearance, and has remained a favourite plant of mine.

The trouble with the garden was the colour of the stone of which the terracing, the balustrades, the steps and the fountains themselves were made. My changes in the planting did something to cool things down, but the stonework remained. Cecil Beaton was particularly unkind about it: though he thoroughly enjoyed (and who would not?) the food and comfort of staying with the Viceroy. He did not admire the stonework, although I had done much to hide it with evergreens – which also gave some colour in the 'dead' season and softened the colours of the planting. The stone he described as 'pig-pink' and 'opaque as plasticine, retaining the heat of the day, and throwing it out, angrily, at dusk'.

Several special features of the garden must be mentioned – some practical, some showing that touch of fantasy that Sir Edwin Lutyens knew so well how to give. The central lawn, generously proportioned, offered the perfect setting for the vast garden parties the Viceroy had to hold. The circular, tiered sunk garden, surrounding a lotus-strewn pool, when in full flush of flower, must be one of the great sights of the gardening world. Robert Byron, years ago, described 'skeleton towers of stone in the four corners of the garden, to whose outline, trees, when grown, will be cut so as to leave doors and windows in their midst'. 'When grown' ... when I was in Delhi in 1943 and 1944 the trees had not quite filled out their allotted framework, but the 'skeleton towers' combined with foliage, presented romantic, Piranesi-like, outlines. The pergolas of the garden are fantastic, shaped in obelisks and hoops of stone, and swagged, not only with roses, jasmine and vines, but with the strongly scented goblets of *Mandevilla suaveolens*, a Chilean creeper of great beauty.

Under one terrace ran a cool dusky walk, one wall of which was curtained (when one of the ninety gardeners had remembered to turn the tap) with falling water.

Water, the Orientals say, is the music of the garden. In the garden of the Rashtrapati Bhavan it certainly plays an all-important part. There are even fountains crowning the cornice of the Palace's garden façade. When I was in charge of the water works, they were never turned on, but to mark an evening party on the floodlit lawn, for over a thousand guests, to celebrate the end of the war with Japan, I could not resist giving the order for once, to make them play. The result was unfortunate, and one of the stateroom ceilings caved in.

Under the rule of the Moguls, great rulers and nobles delighted in gardens planted with scented flowers, and fenced with fretted marble, as can be seen in many Rajput paintings of the day; it was the British who brought their simple garden skills to India. They taught them to their *malis* (gardeners), many of whom were eager pupils and proved natural gardeners. For 150 years the British gardened in India, and gardens surrounded the simplest and most isolated bungalow (from the Hindi word meaning 'in the style of Bengal'). The Rashtrapati Bhavan is far from being an isolated bungalow, it is a great palace; the only palace built anywhere this century. It is good to know that the unique garden which it overlooks is kept up very much as it has always been.

Opposite above Water flows over intricately carved stone steps. *Below* Shade, always important in Oriental gardens, is provided by meticulously clipped Ashok trees (*Saraca indica*), known in India as the Sorrowless, as Buddha is said to have been born in the shade of one. *Above right* What the well-known writer Robert Byron described as 'skeleton towers of stone' stand at each corner of the Mogul garden, veiled in greenery. *Below right* Lutyens loved the sound and sparkle of water.

Opposite The fountains of the garden play a dominant role. Their outline was inspired by the giant leaf pads of the *Victoria regia* waterlily. *Right* Lutyens's dome, reflected in the deeper blue of one of the canals which traverse the garden, challenging the azure Indian sky.

MAURITIUS

An island with one of the finest of Botanic Gardens

Mauritius, though known by name all over the world, is extremely small, about the same size as Surrey in England. Its mild climate all the year round, light but regular rainfall and its varied terrain – mountain, virgin forest (less of that than there was, alas) and fertile plains – make for an animal and vegetable population of great variety.

The island's story, short but eventful, can be quickly told. Discovered by the Portuguese in 1505, Mauritius was occupied by the Dutch at the end of the sixteenth century, who found it totally uninhabited: so there are really no native Mauritians. Everyone is an immigrant to some degree, including, unfortunately for the animal and bird population of the island, imported dogs, cats, monkeys, mongooses and rats. The island's strategic value to European powers lay in its being on the sea route to India. The Dutch stayed on for 120 years, but left few constructive traces when they abandoned the island in 1710. The French moved in five years later, and were there for ninety-five years. During their tenure they left an indelible imprint. French is still more widely spoken than English, though both are taught in schools: and all Mauritians, Indians, Chinese and Créoles alike, have an attractive French air about them.

There are several fascinating gardens in Mauritius, by far the most interesting being the Royal Botanic Gardens at Pamplemousses. It was a perfect Mauritian day when I was shown these famous gardens by Mr Amin Osman of the Ministry of Agriculture. Huge flocculent clouds floated in the cobalt sky. We entered the gardens through rather pompous looking white cast-iron gates, set in heavy railings – very English, though they were a gift to the gardens by a Frenchman, and the gates are said to have won a prize at the Crystal Palace Exhibition.

A complete tour, plant by plant, of the garden at Pamplemousses would take too much space, but one of the high spots, for professional or amateur visitors alike, must surely be the impressive Poivre Avenue, leading to the right soon after the entrance gates – two soaring lines of that beautiful tree, the Royal Palm. Further on and to the right lies the waterlily pond, shown overleaf.

Two beautiful plants in the Pamplemousses gardens caught my eye: a dazzling orange climber, *Butea frondosa superba*, shown on the next page, and the charming *Petrea volubilis*, with its blue flowers on long sprays.

Of great interest to the casual visitor are the plants one sees all over Mauritius, when driving along the excellent, if winding, roads of the island, among them the pale pink, cream-coloured and pearly white bougainvilleas – so much more alluring than the more usual strident purple variety – and the ivory-flowered allamandas.

Opposite The flower-filled garden of Le Réduit, the Governor's Residence, has the dramatic range of the Moka mountains for background.

A plantsman's playground

Opposite In the famous Botanic Garden at Pamplemousses is this celebrated waterlily pond, one of the most famous in the world, where the water is almost completely covered with the giant foliage of the *Victoria regia* lily. This has flowers which open white, and fade to pink. It was first induced to flower outside its native Brazil by Sir Joseph Paxton (1801–65), architect of the Crystal Palace in London, in a greenhouse specially built for it in the Duke of Devonshire's garden at Chatsworth in Derbyshire, England in 1849. *Above* Among the fascinating plants to be seen flourishing in the Botanic Garden of Pamplemousses is *Butea frondosa superba*, called after the Earl of Bute, a great patron of botany in the eighteenth century. With the Princess of Wales, he greatly encouraged the foundation of Kew Gardens, which has contributed so enormously to botany and horticulture all over the world. Butea has flowers which are papilionaceous, that is, they are supposed to have the form of butterflies. In its native country, India, it is known as the Dhak tree. *Above right* Government House, built in the eighteenth century for the French governors of the island, has an extensive *potager*, with a 'cutting garden', here shown against a background of palm trees, and the brilliant blue sky and dazzling white clouds of Mauritius. *Below right* A nave of that most beautiful of all palm trees – the Royal Palm (*Roystonea regis*). Roystonea's pearly white boles can grow to a height of 60 feet (18 metres) and can make an enfilade of truly royal proportions. The benevolent climate of Mauritius provides ideal growing conditions.

SOUTH AFRICA

Fairest gardens in 'the fairest Cape'

Sir Francis Drake, when his ship touched at the Cape in June 1580, was so struck by the extraordinary flora that he found, as well as by the spectacular beauty of the landscape, that he called it 'The Fairest Cape in the circumference of the Earth'.

Over 400 years later, one of the finest of all botanic gardens is to be found at Kirstenbosch. Kirstenbosch (the word means cherry orchard) is unlike any other botanic garden in that it only grows plants indigenous to South Africa. Most other botanic gardens – Kew included – delight in growing exotic plants from other lands. The Kirstenbosch policy is not dictated in any way by xenophobia, but by the fact that the South African flora is absolutely unique. In an area about the size of the Isle of Wight, there grows a variety of plants known as the Fynbos ('fine bush') richer than in any similar area anywhere.

A Director of Kirstenbosch, Brian Rycroft, tells us in his distinguished book about the garden, that in the Cape Peninsula 'more than 2,600 recorded species cover the land in an intricate blending of form, colour, size and shape. The diversity of the plants makes the area one of intense interest and importance to scientists, and a mine of floral treasures for the gardener and landscape artist'. In the conclusion to the Introduction to his book he sums up with an apt quotation from Douglas Jerrold's *The Wild Garden*. 'A garden is a beautiful book, writ by the finger of god; every flower and every leaf is a letter. You have only to learn them.'

Kirstenbosch is a scientific and educational institution, but it maintains an intimate association with the public in many of its activities. Men and women come from far and wide to visit Kirstenbosch, to study here and to enjoy its beauty and peace, the sanctuary created in the turmoil of modern living.

The Peninsula is so special, and so unlike any other area of the same size, not only in Africa, but in the whole world, that it is no wonder that Sir Francis was impressed. Some of the beautiful plants that grow in this much favoured garden we show on the next pages. Most were photographed at Kirstenbosch.

But beautiful flowers and striking vegetation are not confined to Cape Province. In Natal, hundreds of miles away but still in South Africa, the native flora is as astonishingly opulent and luxuriant. Lying nearer the equator, the climate is almost, though not quite tropical, and there one can find exotic trees, such as those in the splendid, many coloured garden of Amanzimnyama (pages 68–71). Distances in South Africa are so immense that one forgets; Amanzimnyama is near Durban and Durban is 600 miles (965 km) from Cape Town, as is Mr and Mrs Fleetwood Tucker's charming, much smaller garden at Ifafa (page 67).

Opposite The pale orange, thistle-like flowers of one of the most beautiful of South African plants, leucospermum, are caught in the rays of the early morning sun. Beyond, the dramatic outline of a spur of Table Mountain.

Kirstenbosch – one of the truly great botanic gardens

Above In the garden at Kirstenbosch, rising from a carpet of mesembryan-themum and dimorphotheca, the spiky outlines of tall aloes are silhouetted against the lake.

Opposite above Much of the drama of the garden at Kirstenbosch derives from its mountainous setting and its perpetual canopy of blue sky and quickly moving snowy clouds. In this picture a bright sheet of daisy-flowered *Dorotheanthus bellidiflorus*, very much a native of Cape Province, wraps a low outcrop of rock. *Opposite left* A luxuriant cluster of that native plant of South Africa, the rich orange clivia, named after a Duchess of Northumberland whose maiden name was Lady Charlotte Clive. Clivias grow from bulbs, and their glossy leaves are evergreen. *Centre Leucodendron argentium*, the silver tree, is one of the jewels of the Cape flora, and unique to that area. It is difficult to convey its true beauty in a photograph, but its argent leaves against the blue sky are unforgettable. *Right* Cactus of every kind flourish in South Africa, as does prickly pear, though this has never become a menace as it did in Australia.

Rustenberg – a garden with an English air near Stellenbosch

A quite different scene to that of the fabulous Kirstenbosch, but extraordinarily charming in its own way, is the garden at Rustenberg where Mrs Pat Barlow has created, in not many years, a most beautiful set-piece. It is in the romantic Ida's Valley, and is a garden very much in the classic English tradition, planted on an impressive scale and in perfect taste. The wall and terraces are of local stone, built with the help of Italian prisoners of war between 1940 and 1945. The garden comprises many typically English features with splendid views towards the nearby mountains. There are sunk gardens scented with lavender and pungent with the spicy smell of herbs and clipped santolina: terraces set with carnations and phlox, plants which are happy growing in paving, 'flowers beneath the foot', but not seeming to mind.

The scent of different thymes fills the clean South African air. There is a water garden, complete with the exotic leaves of *Gunnera manicata* from Brazil, and surrounded with a kaleidoscopic border of native flowers of every colour, spiked with the scarlet of *Lobelia cardinalis*. One wall of the house itself is curtained by the white sprays of wisteria.

Opposite In one garden, walled for protection from breezes from the nearby mountains which flank Ida's Valley. Herb-like plants with scented leaves cluster in the beds centred on a terracotta urn. A leafy trellis makes a screen for a Victorian fern leaf seat, such as one might find in many gardens, say, in Sussex. *Above* A white wisteria creates a Japanese pattern of shadows on the whitewashed walls of Mrs Barlow's house. What in Scotland is called a craw-stepped gable is typical of Cape Dutch architecture. Wisteria got its name from Caspar Wistar (1761–1818), a Professor at the University of Pennsylvania. *Right* Brilliant shrub colour in a closely planted border.

Above Perfectly rounded mounds of close-cropped box contrast with silver cushions of Cotton Lavender (*Santolina incana*) in the snugly walled garden at Rustenberg. *Left* A well-laid stair carpet of Cape daisies (*Bellis mucronatus*), leads up to the terrace. *Opposite* Wisteria and an Italian lemon jar.

A garden in the luxuriant climate of Natal, just over a mile from the sea

Mr and Mrs Fleetwood Tucker's farm lies in hilly countryside surrounded by sugar cane and indigenous bush. It is over 300 feet (91 metres) above sea level with a beautiful view of the Ifafa Lagoon and the Indian Ocean.

All flowers are favourites with Shannon Tucker, but she especially likes all daisies: the shaggy Shasta daisy (*Chrysanthemum maximum*), the new double yellow daisy (*Chrysanthemum frutescens*), and, especially, the little kingfisher daisy (*Felicia rotundifolia*), which is indigenous to South Africa. Then, says Mrs Tucker, 'I love all our flowering trees, four especially: *Cassia fistula* (Shower of Gold, or Indian laburnum), very similar to an English laburnum, and the pink form, *Cassia javanica*, the pink *Tibouchina glandulosa* from South America, the yellow and mauve tabebuia from New Zealand, and the elegant leopard tree (*Caesalpinia ferrae*), so called because the bark is spotted like a leopard.'

Ideally, she admits, she would have loved a typical English country garden, but is pleasantly surprised by the number of English plants that can be grown. 'I have come to love the exotic colourful foliage which suits this climate, and have just started a shady indigenous section, all in soft variations of green, to contrast with the other bright leaves around.'

Other good plants in the Tucker garden are the blue *Salvia farinacea* which is quick growing, hardy and a continuous flowerer, Barberton daisies, white and pink hibiscus, variegated oleanders, and, of course, bougainvilleas.

Opposite above Red Barberton daisies, a kind of gerbera, revel in the sharply drained condition provided by a low dry wall. *Below left* A feature of many Natal gardens is the taste for contrast in foliage. *Right* A more showy cousin of the Amaryllis, *Furcraea gigantea*, makes an explosion of leaves. *Above* Rich leaves and bright flowers. Vibrant crotons and cannas in the foreground, and a distant view of the Indian Ocean. *Below* Another furcraea, yuccas, and dimorphotheca with a bougainvillea beyond.

Amanzimnyama – the most spectacular garden in Natal, visited by thousands every year

Amanzimnyama lies in a countryside of sugar-cane fields, about three-quarters-of-an-hour's drive up the coast from Durban. The name Amanzimnyama is the Zulu word for 'dark water', and the property derives its name from the black waters of a stream from the working of a nearby sugar-mill, long since in disuse. Water is a feature of this lushly-planted garden, which is open to the public every day.

All year round, the garden is full of interest and colour, for plants grow exuberantly in the subtropical climate of Natal; their flowers and leaves vie with each other to take the eye with their brilliant tints. Bougainvilleas offer every shade of crimson and purple; there are groves of strelitzias, not only of the usual size, but also in the form of trees, allamandas with flowers like golden trumpets and heliconias with flowers like lobster claws. These, and a hundred other flowers of the semi-tropics, thrive beside such homely English flowers as marigolds and anemones.

Above Close to the crisply painted house is a pergola hung about with a cloud of the blue flowers of *Petrea volubilis* – *Petrea* after Lord Petre, an eighteenth-century patron of botany, and *volubilis*, which means twisting round. *Below* Strelitzia was named after Queen Charlotte of England, wife of George III, and born a Princess of Mecklenberg-Strelitz. Colloquially it is called the Bird of Paradise flower from the odd formation of its petals. In the picture, strelitzia rises from an undergrowth of scarlet kalanchoes. *Opposite above* Duck houses on a specially constructed island. In the background, *Bougainvillea natalia*, called after Natal Province. *Below* In front of the house, in a natural dell, a bow-shaped balustrade overlooks the ornamental pool, with its rocks and exotic foliage.

Above left A lone Royal Palm rises above the many varied shrubs of Amanzimnyama's garden. *Above right* In a raised bed of brickwork, a bold planting of deep red kalanchoes. *Above* The yellow candles of *Pachystachys lutea*, an exotic cousin of the acanthus. The red-leaved plant is acalypha, a form of euphorbia. *Left* A miniature cascade finds its way down a green grown slope. *Opposite* Rich and varied foliage and the early early blue flowers of a *Jacaranda jasminoides*.

NORTH AFRICA

The garden of a house called Star of Venus, in Tunisia

The actual name, in Arabic, of Baroness Edwina d'Erlanger's beautiful house is Nejma Ezzohra, 'Star of Venus'. The Baroness has recently put much effort into the garden, which originally was laid out by her mother-in-law, Baroness Rodolphe d'Erlanger.

The present Baroness's son writes of his mother's home: 'When the site was purchased, it was no more than red sandstone rock, with three eucalyptus trees.

'It took ten years to build the house, now recognized as a superb example of Arab architecture. My grandfather only employed the finest craftsmen, from both Tunisia and Morocco.'

The site itself, according to legend, was the site of Hamilcar's palace (Hamilcar being the father of Hannibal). Excavation is said to have worn out 10,000 picks and shovels. St Louis, legend again has it, took the name of Sidi-Bou-Saïd during his Arab crusade. So, the present house and garden is not only beautiful, but has historic, and even Saintly associations.

The garden once extended all the way down to the sea, and covered 20 acres of terraces. It needed twenty-five gardeners: this must have been an uphill struggle (no pun intended) for there were free running gazelles, a gift from the famous El Glaoui, and white peacocks at liberty, which ate many of the newly planted shrubs and trees. The gazelles and peacocks were in turn eaten by the German and Italian forces who occupied the house during the Second World War: and perhaps this made present-day upkeep somewhat easier.

The occasional pines, some growing at crazy angles as a result of a

Left Oranges mingle with bougainvillea below a nearby window overlooking the garden. *Opposite* The Persian garden, with shaded loggia.

tornado, palms and monkey-puzzle trees underplanted with geraniums, hibiscus, iris and violets, and with jasmine or bougainvillea growing up them, take away any feeling of symmetry. In Tunis, they say that symmetry is a mark of perfection which belongs only to Allah. The smells in the evening are magical, particularly at orange blossom time.

Today most of the lower terraces going down to the sea have been left to go back to nature, and have become the domain of hares, partridges, hoopoes, and bee eaters. Only the upper terraces are still cultivated, and are themselves mini-terraced for irrigation purposes. They are like the hanging gardens of Babylon on a small scale, and are planted with pink hanging geraniums and jasmine. When in flower, the scent is intoxicating.

Dotted around, are, of course, olive trees, almonds, palms, cypresses and eucalyptus, with cicadas singing loudly in them all in hot weather.

Above Low balustrading, flowers and greenery. *Opposite above* Paving of inlaid stone. *Below left* A flower-framed terrace. *Below right* An urn with yellow jasmine.

A Moroccan medley of flowers

A small house (*overleaf*), smothered in flowers inside and out has been the home in Tangier of an Englishman, the Hon. David Herbert, for forty years. No one knows better than he the ins and outs of gardening in Morocco. He grows eighteen different sorts of hibiscus, and oleanders in shades of pink, white, salmon and apricot, heavily scented hedychium (their name means sweet snow) and rampant ruby-coloured Morning Glories. Mr Herbert's sister

specially recalls a magic moment in spring when the bougainvillea, wisteria and jasmine were all in flower at once. Part of the garden is hedged in lantana.

Magnolia grandiflora and *delavayii* are the only two magnolias which condescend to open their pale flowers but must surely be two of the best. Roses make a riot of colour and scent for months on end, and grow so well that they have to be pruned three times a year. Daturas offer yellow and red

trumpets as well as the more usual white. *Bauhinia galpinii* offers flowers as exotic as orchids and edible leaves as ugly as camels' feet. In fact, some people call it the camel's foot tree. The RHS *Dictionary of Gardening* describes its unlovely foliage as 'connate with an awn in the recess', whatever that means. However, it makes a handsome shrub, and is much admired. Mr Herbert admits few garden failures. 'Everything grows, really.'

But as there is no dormant season to speak of, plants in Morocco – herbaceous plants – are not happy at the thought of a twelve-month flowering year. And plants grown from bulbs such as scillas and tulips are occasionally attacked by 'horrible little insects with life-size lobster claws, with which they bite the biggest bulbs in half'.

In a charming little aviary, Mr Herbert keeps brightly coloured birds with exotic names: calypsos and cockateels, rosellas, red-beaked parakeets and Peruvian lovebirds. A nearby bougainvillea rather clashes with the red parrots.

When Dot and Dash, Mr Herbert's two kittens, approach the aviary, wanting to be friendly, the lovebirds greet them with rude words in, presumably, Peruvian dialect.

Above Embowered in bougainvillea.
Below A guest house for fine feathered friends.

The public gardens of Chaouen
present a picture of peace

Chaouen is in the Rif and its name means 'two peaks' from the white mountains above it. Once a holy city, the first infidel to enter Chaouen was a London *Times* correspondent, William Harris, early this century, who had heard of the beauty of the local women. Besides female beauties, Chaouen produces revolutionaries, like the famous Abdul Krim, captured finally by Franco in the Rif war; and also the plotters of a recent assassination attempt on King Hassan.

Above Arches of evergreen, and *right*, a fish fountain cools the warm Moroccan air.

La Palmeraie – exotic plants arranged by an artist's hand

The gardens of La Palmeraie in Marrakesh were laid out about 1922 by the well-known French artist Jacques Majorelle. They are arranged, strange as it may seem, rather on Anglo-Saxon lines, with paths bordered not with delphiniums and rose trees, but with succulents and palm trees. The perceptive visitor soon sees how effective such a planting is, for with their glaucous leaves and sculptural outline, succulents provide exactly the contrast in form that a well-planned border needs.

When I visited the garden, the *Aloe arborescens* were in full orange flower, and the box-edged beds fairly spilled over with bright sedums, and the scarlet cox-combs

of *Erythrina crista-galli*, the Coral Bush. What was particularly striking to the London visitor were the spreading bushes of impatiens, as large as rhododendrons, in pink and red and white – the good natured Busy Lizzie of so many office window sills.

The Palmeraie is one of the sights of Marrakesh. But rather than the plants themselves, it is the way Jacques Majorelle assembled them, with his special eye for contrast and grouping, which is instructive to any imaginative gardener.

Opposite A Moroccan kiosk bridges a canal. *Top* The soaring orange candelabra of *Aloe arborescens* frame an arched

gateway. *Above* Silver-leaved Bismarckia palm trees spread their fronds above scarlet sedums.

PORTUGAL

Blue and white tiles and flowers of every colour, under the Lusitanian sun

Portugal, which Lord Byron called a 'purple land where law secures not life' is now as law-abiding – or more so – as Tunbridge Wells or Newport.

Portugal's most beautiful garden, and it has many, must be at the former Royal Palace of Queluz, which lies about nine miles (15 km) north of Lisbon, on the way to the charming 'hill-station' of Sintra, where the Portuguese say that 'summer goes to spend the winter'. Below the pink rococo walls of the palace is one of the most exquisite gardens in the world. The palace itself was built in the mid-eighteenth century – and was lived in by the Portuguese royal family until the revolution of a few years ago. It is still partly occupied, and on occasions provides accommodation for distinguished guests of the government, such as Queen Elizabeth II and Prince Philip.

The builder of the palace was Don Pedro, second son of Don João V, who married his niece Queen Maria, and how happy they must have been in their beautiful new home. Fortunately the great Lisbon earthquake of 1755 had not unduly held up the work.

The gardens were designed in part by a Frenchman, Jean Baptiste Robillon, and are French in feeling – though the exuberance and frivolity of the statues and garden ornaments, so different from the cold, ordered classicism of, say, Versailles, remind the visitor that he is not in France. The frilled and furbelowed sphinxes and, of course, the *Azulejos*, the blue and white tiles, make Portuguese gardens distinctly different from any others in the world. The hedges are quite extraordinary – box seems to grow in Portugal as it does nowhere else in Europe – slowly, but so strongly, that they say (I have never tried) that one can actually sit on it. It was between such low, impeccably trimmed greenery, that in 1786 the slightly deranged Queen Joaquina is said to have commanded William Beckford to run races with her ladies in waiting: how bored he must have been.

The great allure of Queluz might be summed up in two words: grandeur and naïvety. I first heard of the palace and its gardens in a letter I received in India, when I was stationed momentarily in a particularly depressing town made up mostly of military cantonments. My correspondent was a well-known writer with powers of vivid description; he was in Lisbon en route for Washington. The picture he painted of Queluz with its fountains, its elegant frivolity and its rosy rococo architecture might have come in a missive, not from another world but another epoch.

No description of Portuguese gardens would be complete without a special word about *Azulejos*. They are said, originally, to have come from Delft, but I have never seen them used in Holland as they are in Portugal.

Opposite The former Royal Palace of Queluz overlooking the garden with its massive box hedges. The borders are planted with red leaved iresine.

They make the beauty of many Portuguese gardens, and not only gardens. The interiors of churches and private houses are often decorated with them as well. They are usually blue and white, but occasionally, as at Queluz they are to be found in other colours, where they are spectacularly employed to depict historical scenes, sea battles and royal pageants.

Fronteira

Azulejos are a hallmark of Portuguese gardens, but nowhere, not even in the splendid pleasuregrounds of the Royal Palace of Queluz, are they to be seen in more beauty than in the garden of Fronteira, which lies almost in the suburbs of Lisbon. The Quinta do Fronteira is a century older than Queluz. The tilework there is less sophisticated, but more robust, less influenced by Versailles, more truly Portuguese. That Fronteira exists at all is in itself extraordinary, for on 2 November ('The Day of the Dead') 1755, most of the great quintas in the area were destroyed by the famous Lisbon earthquake. Perhaps, because it was older and more sturdily built, the Quinta do Fronteira survived: and there it is today – a miracle of faded blue and white beauty, embowered in scarlet geraniums, with its immaculate patterns of box hedging stretching towards the surrounding garden walls, and, alas, the ever-encroaching factory buildings and tall chimneys of Lisbon's busy suburb Benfica, home of one of the world's most famous football teams.

As the expectant visitor enters the garden at Fronteira, he comes on a wide parterre, 250 feet (66 metres) square, quartered by four broad paths, and with a fountain for centrepiece, and unfortunately not the most beautiful fountain one has ever seen, and surely a later addition. But the chief beauty and great feature of the garden is the great tank with its imposing flight of steps and arched niches depicting Portuguese heroes of long ago.

Their story is worth the telling. Although, for 400 years, Portugal has been the devoted ally of England, there have

Above 'Frilled and furbelowed sphinxes'. *Below* Trophies of arms and statues against the bluest of skies. *Opposite* Reflections in the canal at Queluz. The steep tiled walls are capped with flower-filled urns.

been rifts, if not very serious ones, in that long playing lute. In the fourteenth century, John of Gaunt's daughter, Philippa, became engaged to marry the then King of Portugal and afterwards became the mother of one of Portugal's most illustrious sons, Henry the Navigator. Twelve noble Portuguese maidens were sent from Portugal to escort the English princess to Lisbon.

So far, so good. But while in England the Portuguese maidens were insulted by the too ardent advances of the boorish young men of the English Court, and they returned with the Princess to Portugal, full of tales of their bad treatment. Whereupon, twelve Portuguese knights set out for England to avenge their countrywomen's honour. There are the knights fashionably armoured, portrayed in the tiled panels in the garden at Fronteira: and Portugal's greatest poet Camoens described them thus in his celebrated work 'The Lusiads':

With arms and uniforms on latest plan
With helmets, crests, devices, gems of art
Horses, and all that colour could impart.

History does not tell us the outcome of their gallant adventure. But the garden at Fronteira is a fit setting for such a romantic story.

The garden visitor does not go to Fronteira to look for rare plants. If he does, he will be disappointed. But what he will find is a garden, not so grand as that at the Palace of Queluz, but, with its blue and white tiles, its fountains and its veridian pools, a garden unique in the spell it casts.

Above A monumental bridge with different coloured *azulejos* at Queluz. *Below* Fronteira – fountains and a palm tree in a garden laid out in box. *Opposite* The blue and white tile-walled tank at Fronteira – with equestrian portraits of the famous twelve knights.

Fragile magic at the Quinta do Vinagre

Some years ago I was asked to help, by my friends Monsieur and Madame Pierre Schlumberger, not to redesign, but to elaborate their very beautiful Portuguese garden: that of the Quinta do Vinagre near Colares. All the ready-made assets which a garden designer welcomes were already there. Eighteenth-century terraces, a shining river – the Colares – running through the garden, a rare thing to find in Portugal, with two eighteenth-century or earlier bridges across it. An accomplished Paris garden architect – and a friend of mine – Mogens Tvede, had already done much to beautify this lovely pleasureground. In four telling words, which every gardener will understand, the bones were there.

I set to work. We conjured an English rose garden with 500 roses, a mixed shrub and herbaceous border (with interesting plants imported from England) along the river's bank, a flight of steps, of simple wood, up a tree-clad incline, planted on either side with silver plants. All very pretty and very successful, and a little frivolous.

Most frivolous of all, was an aviary of blue *azulejos* with artificial birds of brightly coloured pottery, made by a clever girl at a London art school. In its heyday – which only lasted a few years – the garden at the Quinta do Vinagre was a place of magic, perfectly maintained by an army of gardeners.

Then, overnight, misfortune. A drastic change of regime in Portugal, hardly worthy of the name of a revolution, certainly caused changes. A fire, which might never have happened if the house had been fully staffed, destroyed much of the interior of the Quinta itself. The garden workforce was seriously reduced. The newly created pleasuregrounds were converted to citrus orchards. Laudable, but sad for me. Then worst of all, after fire, another element attacked. Water. The Colares river flooded, as it had not done for centuries: the river walls were washed away, as were the bridges, over which Byron and Beckford had once ridden (and described). Carefully nurtured, imported trees were uprooted.

Curiously, the most light-hearted addition of all, the aviary, survived both fire and flooding.

The third element, air, has yet to strike. Never the sturdiest of structures, or meant to be, one day I may be told that my little aviary has been blown away. But I do hope not.

Above left In the courtyard of the Quinta do Vinagre, a raised tank is fed by a lion fountain. *Below left* White peacocks, one with tail outspread, at Fort Saint George, above Lisbon. *Above* The aviary of pottery birds which survived the flooding. *Opposite* Citrus orchards have replaced herbaceous borders.

Above left In the garden at Sintra of the Marquesa de Cadaval is this elegantly windowed garden pavilion, with typically Portuguese fenestration, pediment and balustrade. The whole façade is of blue and white *Azulejos*.
Below left Many English and Americans have houses in Portugal, so Anglo-Saxon influences are manifest in many of the gardens they have planted there. Here, that most English of roses, 'Mermaid', child of *Rosa bracteata* and an unknown double yellow tea rose, revels in the Lusitanian sunlight, wreathing the balustrade of a neatly laid terrace. Portuguese masons excel at such work.
Above In the garden of the Quinta do Vinagre, set against a background of dusky evergreens, a lead vase with an artificial plant with gilded leaves. *Opposite above* Janus-headed busts, each looking two ways at once, in a setting of greenery in the garden of a villa in Sintra. *Below left* At the entrance to the villa are several elements of Portuguese outdoor art. Delicate iron scrolled-work handrails cast their shadow on finely laid paving in a setting once more of *Azulejos*.
Below right A famous Portuguese garden, part of it dating from the Moorish occupation, at Bacalhoa. The Quinta and the garden have been restored with immense taste by a munificent American woman.

Madeira, a Portuguese island with the kindest of gardening climates

At the Quinta do Palheiro do Ferreiro, which means the Quinta of the Thatched Cottage of the Blacksmith, the Blandy family, long resident on the island, have over the years created a famous garden. Madeira has an almost perfect climate for gardens; frost is unknown and there is water everywhere. Even at the end of October, there seemed to be masses of flowers still giving of their best everywhere; not only the ubiquitous bougainvillea and hydrangeas, but roses, blue plumbago, daturas and trumpeted mandevillas.

The house was built in 1891 in a pleasing mixture of English and Portuguese styles, and is set in a truly magnificent garden. The trees were extraordinary. A tulip tree (*Liriodendron tulipifera*) near the house was all of 60 feet (18 metres) high, and only sixty-six years old.

Among the star attractions pointed out to me were a bed of proteas, from South Africa, in full luxuriance of growth, *P. compacta* and *P. cynaroides* among them. Elsewhere in the garden was an impressive clump of *Datura sanguinea* which, I was told, flowered almost all the year round.

Camellias are a feature of the Blandy garden and although when I was there it was October, there were some fine flowers on fifty-year-old bushes of *Camellia sasanqua* – and indeed, the dining-room table was decorated with a silver bowl of these lovely pink and white flowers, a rare table decoration indeed.

Above left Quinta do Palheiro do Ferreiro set in its famous garden. *Below left* The powdery flowers of *Plumbago capensis*. *Below right* Hydrangea paniculata grandiflora in a group with pale pink *Crinum* x *powellii*.

Gibraltar, the garden of Government House, oddly called The Convent

When, some time in the first few years of this century, King Edward VII put in, in the Royal Yacht, to Gibraltar, he was reported in the newspapers as having 'passed two nights at The Convent'. This raised a storm of moral indignation in England. The idea of the King, and the King of Protestant England, too, sleeping in a Convent full of nuns. It was too shocking. Why? How? It seemed unbelievable: but it was easily explained. Government House, Gibraltar, had once been a Convent, and had retained the name. But King Edward, doubtless amused, but always tactful, suggested that it might be better if the name Convent should be dropped, to avoid misunderstandings. Later, I believe at the suggestion of George VI, probably equally amused by the story, the old name was revived.

The garden on which King Edward's bedroom windows looked in those days was very different from the one the visitor to the Convent sees today. I have stayed there twice, once on my way back from India with my wartime chief, Lord Wavell, and once when Sir Gerald Lathbury was Governor. It was Jean, Lady Lathbury, who told me much of the story of the garden.

Until fairly recently, the garden was a formal, and slightly impersonal, affair. Straight paths, ranged on either side with guardsmen – ranks of scarlet geraniums, a few fine trees certainly, but near the house, no cool green lawn, only an arid expanse of dusty gravel.

Since then, successive governors – or their wives – have made many changes, and all for the better: a spreading lawn of a special drought-resistant grass, called in Spanish *gramón*; brimming borders of long-flowering shrubs, such as daturas which bloom for months on end, rare hibiscus, banks of geraniums and pelargoniums in softer shades than pillarbox red, belladonna lilies (*Amaryllis belladonna*) in August, and sweet-smelling freesias in spring. Carnations and lilies brought from England have settled down happily; tulips and daffodils not so successfully.

On my last visit to Gibraltar I spent two happy hours in the garden of the Convent, and in spite of it being October, the garden seemed full of colour and delectable scents. I hope to go again.

Two trees, I specially remember: the first, a handsome evergreen with showy

bracts of flowers in bud, Othonopanax; the second, very famous, and said to be one of the oldest trees in the world – the dragon tree (*Dracaena draco*), seen in the picture above. It is supposed to be over 1,000 years old, and, if so, was growing where it is growing today, long before the Convent was thought of, when the Rock was neither British nor Spanish, but Moorish, and known as Jebel Tariq.

Above Government House, Gibraltar, is officially called the Convent, which it once was. It is set in a flowery garden. One of the most interesting trees leaning into the picture above, is a dragon tree (*Dracaena draco*), which may be 1,000 years old. *Right* A fountain throws up a shining jet of water.

SPAIN

Where the Moors created some of the first gardens in Europe

Spain has some of the most famous gardens in the world, and can certainly be said to have a style of gardening which goes under the name of 'Spanish'. But the most celebrated gardens in Spain, the gardens of the Alhambra and the Generalife, shown on these pages, are really not Spanish at all in conception, but Arabic. It is easy to forget that it was not until the late fifteenth century that Spain became one country. 1492 was a momentous year in world history for it was not only the year that Ferdinand and Isabella's protégé, Christopher Columbus, discovered America, but it was the year their armies finally defeated the Arabs, and expelled them totally from the Iberian Peninsula. Great events, for Granada had been a Moorish province for 700 years; the Spanish dream, that the whole of Spain should be unified, was at last realized. The historian, Agapida, describes Ferdinand of Aragon and his wife Isabella of Castile's entry into the captured city of Granada: 'Equal with each other' [they were both monarchs in their own right] they were raised far above the rest of the world. They appeared, indeed, more than mortal, as if sent by heaven for the salvation of Spain.' But in spite of an aura almost inhuman in its magnificence and glitter, Ferdinand and Isabella were level-headed monarchs. They set about ruling their newly acquired territory and ruling it well. What they found good in the laws that the Arabs left behind, they left unchanged. They had no desire to destroy their palaces, and they found their gardens exactly suited to the climate, as all good gardens should be.

The Moorish roots had struck so deep, that for years their houses and even more, their gardens, not only remained as they had been in the final years of Boabdil, the last Moorish king, but seemed, gradually to become Spanish, though physically they did not change. And of all the gardens in Spain, the gardens of the Alhambra and of the Generalife seem to us today the most Spanish of all, for fortunately they have not changed greatly since the fifteenth century. Gardens, all over the civilized world, depend for their character on the climate, as well as on the mentality and thinking of their creators. In France, Italy and certainly England, gardens were designed as a setting for the house, castle or palace round which they lay. In a sense, building and garden were one. The way of living of the day necessitated that the garden made an extension of the house, and it was but a step for the king, great noble or wealthy landowner, to progress, followed by courtiers, retainers, or his wife, family and dogs, through a garden door, leaving the splendours of tapestries, pictures and gilt-framed pictures to enjoy the equal splendours of terraces, parterres and fountains. There are, at Aranjuez and La Granja, both gardens of royal palaces, pleasuregrounds of the type we describe, but they are not, in essence, Spanish, but draw their inspiration from France. Of Moorish gardens, it has been said that they were planned differently: 'conceived for the retired mode of living of only a small number of inhabitants, for sedentary and contemplative existence'. But in all, whether in palace gardens, in secluded courtyards of private

Opposite It has been said that the Patio de la Riadh, with its arching fountains, is the only garden in Europe to have kept its original fourteenth-century lines.

houses, or in palm-shaded streets and squares, water, and the cool it brings, is always an important element.

Though the refined art of the Moor is very far removed from our mentality and time, the gardens of Granada to this day have kept their patios; the only word that we can recall which Spain has contributed to our modern gardening vocabulary.

Over the centuries, of course, gardens in Spain have changed and foreign influences have made themselves felt, and fashion has had its say. Some of the gardens we show are not typically Spanish at all, except that most recognize the importance of shade, and the blessing of the sound of falling water.

Opposite The visitor to the Generalife passes through this flower-filled garden, with a central canal bordered with flowers and fresh greenery. The canal itself is planted with a lush line of arum lilies (*Zantedeschia aethiopica*), their roots protected by water from the very occasional frost. *Above* The Court of the Lions, the most famous courtyard of the Alhambra, 'where Mohammedan art surely reaches its peak of beauty'. Of it Professor Moreno has written: 'the stalactitic ornamentation of the ceilings brings to one's mind the structure . . . of a Royal tent . . . in a forest of Palm trees'. *Below* The Fountain of the Lions, dating from the tenth century. An inscription on one of the panels (slightly absurdly) expresses alarm at what the ferocity of the lions might have been, had not respect for the dignity of the Caliph kept them in check. The Courtyard of the Lions is now neatly gravelled: in its Moorish heyday it was surely stood around with pots of lilies, jasmine and sweet-smelling herbs.

A garden of different greens at the Castillo de Santa Clotilde

Half a century ago, just before the Spanish Civil War, the Marqués de Roviralta decided to plan a garden round his new house in Catalonia on the steep shores of the Mediterranean. It needed enterprise and foresight, for the site was not an easy one. It was rocky and precipitous and the surface of the ground had first to be dynamited, then terraced, and tons of good soil imported. Water was not plentiful, and every natural spring had to be utilized. A small army of workmen worked for several years with baskets and wheelbarrows – it was before the days of bulldozers – and slowly a Spanish garden of Eden took shape. Although any mature trees already growing on the site were religiously preserved, hundreds of pines, junipers, crypresses and cedars were brought from other parts of Spain. Pools and fountains were created and an impressive collection of antique statues assembled.

Opposite, right and above John Evelyn in the seventeenth century described his 'garden of curious greenes' and the garden of the Castello de Santa Clotilde in Catalonia is a garden where greenery of every shade makes the overall verdant pattern. On these two pages are a quintet of pictures which show how cypresses, junipers, hollies and cedars, as trees or as clipped hedges, have been used to make a setting for thoughtfully placed sculpture. Particularly to be noted is the way that ivy has been trained to make the risers of a flight of stone steps.

A unique feature of the garden is its proximity to the sea, and the cry of gulls is continually to be heard; as well as the muted sound of children playing on the beach at Blanes, a popular seaside resort less than a mile away. On this, and on the next page, we show pictures of this oasis of verdure on the often sunburnt sea coast of Catalonia. Doña Odalita Roviralta and her family maintain the garden in perfect order. 'It was our father's creation, like we were, and he called it after his wife – Clotilde. I love every tree of it. It is where I am most happy.'

Opposite Santa Clotilde *Top left Acacia canariensis* with ferny leaves and yellow upright bracts of flowers, in the garden at Arucas in the Canary Islands. *Top right* In the Parque del Ouest in Madrid, is one of the best-kept rose gardens in the world, La Rosaleda. The anthracite content in the soil, besides the constant care with which the garden is maintained, produces an astonishing show of roses every summer. *Centre* Mr Anthony Pawson, an Englishman living in Spain, built a house near Alicante in traditional Spanish style, with white walls, and arched loggias for shade. It is set in a flower-filled garden. In spring early buddleia (right-hand corner) scents the air. *Below left* Later in the year one wall is wreathed with pink bignonia. *Right* Nearby, roses open their flowers wide for months on end.

Majorca – gardens in the sun that are never thirsty

George Sand and Chopin, on their unofficial honeymoon in Majorca in 1838, were so unlucky with the weather that at one point the rain came through their roof. That was before they moved to the famous and more waterproof Valldemosa. But the point of the anecdote is that it rained, as it often does in Majorca, the greenest and most fertile of all the Balearic islands. It is not difficult to have a beautiful garden in Majorca, though often the initial construction work presents problems.

In making their garden, shown on this page, on the rocky brink of the ever-blue Mediterranean, Mr and Mrs Ivanovic had to have tons of limestone rock cut away, a truly massive task.

In another part of the island of Majorca, Señor and Señora Bartolomé March have surrounded their beautiful villa, La Torre Sega at Cala Ratjada, with a magnificent garden: the prestigious English garden designer, the late Russell Page had a hand in its plan, and more recently Señor Leandro Silva Delgado. Of the pine trees which give shelter, and retain moisture in the garden Señora March says, 'Their graceful development over the years has been an important factor in the creation of atmosphere'.

Opposite above left The low wall of a terrace in the Ivanovic garden is coped with a luxurious planting of pink ivy-leaved geraniums. The sculpture in the foreground, 'Manifestations II', is by Professor Drago Tršar of the University of Ljubljana in Yugoslavia. *Below left* The garden, which is shaded here and there by native Mediterranean pines, has several flights of steps down to the sea. *Opposite above right* Scarlet hibiscus revel in the Majorcan sun. *Above* At La Torre Sega, broad steps lead down to a wide path in chequerboard paving of sand and faded terracotta, through an enfilade of cypresses. To the right of the picture, square flower-beds in the cutting garden. *Right* A nereid of stone in the shade of a sequestered pool.

Left In a sunlit corner of Señor and Señora March's garden, a palm tree makes a fountain above the lily pond, not of sprays of water, but of its own graceful leaves. Waterlilies respond generously to a place in the sun, as can be seen here, as opposed to the flowers in the more shaded piece of water on the previous page. *Below* Underground lakes, which provide an inexhaustible supply, have made water an important and feasible feature of Majorcan gardens through the centuries. Here in the eighteenth-century garden at Alfabia in a setting of meticulously looked-after palm trees, descending stone steps are balustraded on either side with a series of falling water-jets. These steps probably date from the long Moorish occupation. *Opposite top left* A monumental fountain in the garden at Raixa, surmounted by a gracefully sculpted figure. *Top right* The sound of trickling water on either side soothes the ears of visitors to Raixa as they descend or ascend. *Centre* Cypresses make a wall of green to right and left of a staircase of weathered stone. *Below left* A lion couchant. *Below right Yucca gloriosa*, a noble plant whose original home is in Mexico, flourishes as it might be expected to in Spain and its islands.

ITALY

Splendid pleasuregrounds designed long before any in France or England

In a war dispatch to his brother Pierre de Bourbon about his campaign to seize the Crown of Naples – totally unsuccessful, as it turned out – King Charles VIII of France added a horticultural postscript. The date was 1495 and the King wrote: 'You cannot believe what beautiful gardens I have seen . . . for, on my word, it seems as though only Adam and Eve were wanting to make an earthly Paradise, so full are they of rare and beautiful things'. We do not know which particular gardens so inspired Charles, but we do know that though his campaign was unsuccessful and the gains negligible, the invisible booty he brought back from Italy was of inestimable value – the ideas which were to inspire the Renaissance in art, in architecture, and in the devising of gardens. For Italian gardens were, at that date, infinitely more sophisticated, more extravagant and more imaginative than any in Europe.

One wonders which of the gardens that so impressed the French King have left traces today. At the time of his memorable visit to Italy in 1495, the great Bramante was fifty and at the height of his powers, so it might have been the garden of the Ospedale Maggiore in Milan in which the master had had a hand; or some other pleasureground, such as that at the villa of S. Petraia, where Sangallo (1445–1516) had left his mark. It is difficult to say, because in 1495 many of the masters of Italian garden architecture were children. Just three examples: Raphael Sanzio, who afterwards laid out the garden of the Vatican, was only twelve, Jacopo Sansovino was eight and the celebrated Palladio not yet born.

Many Italian gardens of the early sixteenth century still survive, and the form and feeling of great Italian gardens has altered remarkably little since they so struck Charles's imagination. Fashions in Italian gardens have not gone through the vicissitudes of gardens in, say, England. There has been no sudden craze for topiary – though it was in Italy nearly 2,000 years ago that Pliny the Younger, who wrote volumes on botany, described borders of clipped box at his villa in Tuscany. The 'garden of the intellect' did not greatly appeal to the Italians as it did to French garden architects. In England, especially in the rich Victorian days, ducal seats such as Trentham boasted 'Italian' gardens, with gravelled paths, a dozen statues, not perhaps of the highest quality, and a pompous fountain. They were very different from the real Italian gardens, such as the ones shown here.

Opposite The gardens of the Villa Aldobrandini at Frascati were laid out soon after the villa was built in 1598. The water-garden with its spectacular twin-pillared, water-wreathed fountain was designed by Giovanni Fontana and Orazio Olivieri. It was much admired by John Evelyn in the early seventeenth century. *Right* In the famous Whitaker garden of Malfitano in Palermo, a fountain plays its slender jets on a moisture-loving philadendron.

The garden of Villa Marlia – once the country palace of Napoleon's sister

Elisa Baciocchi, one of the Emperor Napoleon's three sisters, was a handsome, mannish-looking woman, with a strong will which grew stronger when her all-powerful brother made her Grand Duchess of Tuscany. She ruled her small but rich Grand Duchy with Napoleonic efficiency, and acquired, in 1806, having driven a hard bargain, a country house, La Marlia, near Lucca, which she speedily turned into a Palace.

The seventeenth-century villa was soon converted to suit the current Empire fashion. Adjoining properties were bought, and the garden, though luckily not all of it, was laid out in the smart *jardin anglais* style. Luckily, Elisa's reign ended abruptly when Napoleon fell, and much of the garden, including the enchanting *Teatro di Verdura*, survived as did the pebble-work *frontone*, which shelters a marble statue of Leda in decorous conversation with a swan.

The garden of Marlia today is remarkable for its framework of high hedges of ilex and holly, and for its pools and fountains, balustraded in time-mellowed stone and set against a background of greenery. There is also that feature of so many Italian gardens, the *Giardino dei Limoni*, the Lemon Garden, with pots of swagged and decorated terracotta.

Elisa was not a bad woman; one of her constructive occupations while Grand Duchess was to revive the fortunes of the Carrara marble quarries, which soon gained a European reputation.

Opposite Golden-flowered lantana growing happily in a traditionally swagged terracotta pot by the pool. *Top* On a balustrade a line of pots of different plants, with blue-flowered *Plumbago capensis*, a native of South Africa. *Centre left* A small formal garden with silver-leaved helichrysum hedges, enclosing symmetrical areas of powdered brick. *Centre right* A trio of white marble urns from the nearby Carrara marble quarries, which fortunes were revived by the enterprising Elisa's patronage. *Below* Like so many gardens in Italy, Marlia has its *Giardino dei Limoni*, with rows of lemon trees in serried lines.

Left As in many old Italian gardens there are in the garden at Marlia imposing architectural features, some, it is said, the work of the great Filippo Juvara (1676–1736). Here a high *frontone* of different coloured stone provides a niche for a statue of Leda and her swan. *Above* The rich – sometimes too rich – colouring of bougainvillea, with a vase of the softer-toned blue plumbago. *Opposite* In the garden of La Mortola, there are many paths such as this one, running between banks brimful with a rich planting of shrubs. In the foreground, the blue spires of *Echium fastuosum*.

La Mortola – a great garden, created by an English family over a hundred years ago, is given over to Italian care

The history of the celebrated garden at La Mortola, near Ventimiglia, in Italy, can really be said to have begun in 1867, when Sir Thomas Hanbury – great-grandfather of the present owner – saw the property from the sea and recognised, in spite of the barren and almost treeless terrain, the place's great possibilities as a garden. The *palazzo* was in ruins: the sky could be seen through the ceiling of the *salone*, but the capabilities of the site – as Lancelot Brown might have said a century before – were certainly there.

The setting was beautiful, with the blue Mediterranean lapping the rocks below, and the mountains beyond. There were a few old trees which had been tough enough to withstand the occasional gale and continual salt spray. Frost was little known, and never more severe than four or five degrees, and seldom lasting more than a few hours. The local saint, San Mauro al Barbo Bianco, was generally said to be kind, and though he occasionally

dusted the surrounding slopes with snow, he more usually brought refreshing rain. But the soil presented problems, as it was poor and calcareous, which many plants dislike. It would be no good trying to grow rhododendrons or azaleas, and only a few magnolias ever condescended to survive in it, the Italian native *M. grandiflora* being one. The surface of the soil was ugly – white chalk, streaked muddy brown. Much later in the story of the garden, constant care was taken to hide this with groundcovering plants like lamium, and the natural undergrowth of the maquis, such as thyme, myrtle, prostrate juniper and rosemary.

Sir Thomas Hanbury was greatly helped in the creation of the garden by his brother Daniel, a noted botanist, who through his connections in the botanical world did much to establish the garden at

Above left The garden was restored almost from complete dereliction in the last quarter of the nineteenth century. *Below left* Aloes, with their fleshy glaucous leaves and bright heads of flowers are a feature at La Mortola. One *A. hanburyana* is named for the Hanbury family. *Above* Oranges glisten above the lilac blue flower heads of *Scilla peruviana*.

La Mortola as a home for rare plants from all over the world – not only a place of celebrated beauty, but a centre of learning and instruction, too.

Just a few of the more interesting trees and plants in the garden are a giant eucalyptus, one of the first Hanbury-planted trees, drifts of blue *Echium fastuosum*, rich groups of the Hanbury's own aloe, *A. hanburyana*, a 500-year-old carob,

and a cypress avenue, which would grace Frascati.

In early spring, the orange swags of *Bignonia venusta* and the creamy ones of *Clematis armandii* take the eye, and wreaths of Banksian roses, which as every knowledgeable gardener knows, should only be very lightly pruned.

Nearer the *palazzo*, now beautifully restored, are small formal gardens, trimly hedged with lavender and cypress.

Historical postscript: we have already said that the story of the garden began in 1867, but, of course, the history of the place goes back far further. The remains of a Roman road, Via Aurelia, with some of its original paving stones, passes, under high walls, through the garden. A carved inscription tells us that Julius Agricola passed along it in AD 70 on his way to conquer Britain, which he did far more effectively than Julius Caesar, occupying it as far north as the River Tay. He was followed by half-a-dozen historical characters and their trains. These include St Catherine of Siena in June 1376, Macchiavelli in 1511, the Emperor Charles V in 1536 and finally Napoleon in 1796, on his way to his first victories in Italy.

As the late Lady Hanbury once wrote, 'What pictures of history this short list of names calls up.'

Above left White and mauve wisteria wreathe some steps. *Above right* As in so many Italian gardens, the sky line is stabbed with cypresses. *Left* A Japanese lotus vase, with drinking dragon, in a setting of papyrus leaves.

Fontarronco – a garden in Tuscany

The garden at Fontarronco, near Arezzo, is typically Italian but with English undertones. Its owner, Princess Ruffo, has English blood, many English tastes and knows English gardens well – but, for all that, her garden in Tuscany remains delightfully Italian.

Gardeners in Italy have different problems from gardeners in cooler climates. First, very hot summers, and the need for shade; second, they have to water their gardens constantly, or they would have no gardens at all. The Princess's aim is to grow vegetables for the table, and flowers to look at and for cutting, and to devise sitting-out places and shaded walks where she and her guests can escape the heat of the midday sun.

Princess Ruffo is a well-known agriculturist, who has been awarded the Medaglio d'Oro by the Italian government for her successful farming. On her farm she raises a rare kind of cattle, called *Razza chianina*, a breed which was known to the Romans 2,000 years ago and, until recently, had never been exported. Their shining white hides are like satin upholstery, and their black eyes have sweeping eyelashes. They are the greatest help to the Princess in her gardening, obligingly and regularly producing the richest *concime* which goes to fertilize the thin, poor soil.

In summer, the garden at Fontarronco is

full of brilliant colour. Dahlias, asters, chrysanthemums and zinnias show every shade and roses fill the air with their scent. One corner of the garden was planted by an Anglo-Saxon friend with the silver-leaved plants so popular with English gardening connoisseurs today. A large swimming-pool offers coolness, and nearby is a shady arbour, big enough to hold a table and chairs. It is carved out of a Chinese jasmine (*Trachelospermum jasminoides*), a shrub only deigning to survive in the most protected of northern gardens. For some reason trachelospermum, *trachelo* meaning 'neck' in Greek, and *sper-*

mum meaning 'seed', suffers under a double burden of two very cumbersome names. It is also known as rhyncospermum, *rhynco* meaning 'beak'. So either its seeds have necks or are beaked, one can take one's choice. Either way the flowers that produce them smell delicious.

The Princess says that any garden designer would 'make a terrible success in Italy if he could make plans of simple, effective, coloured terraces and small gardens without manpower ... here everyone is mad about flowers without having any notion about what flowers are.' Garden designers in search of 'terrible success', please note.

Opposite The villa Fontarronco.
Above left A green bower, set about with comfortable garden furniture, with walls of white-flowered, sweet-smelling Chinese jasmine. *Above right* An Italian garden would look underfurnished indeed without its pots of citrus fruit. *Below* Brightly coloured gourds drying in the warm sunshine of Tuscany.

GREECE

Terraces overlooking the pale blue (rather than wine dark) Aegean sea

It is said that the Greeks, then at the peak of their aesthetic achievements in architecture and sculpture, were astonished by the beauty and magnificence of the gardens they found when they invaded Persia. Greek poets of that time said little of the beauties of Greek gardens, if indeed any existed, though Homer describes how the home-coming Ulysses, hiding behind a pear tree, watched his old father Laertes hoeing the garden, which was planted with figs, vines and olives.

Though hardly an ideal site for a garden, the arid mountain of Hymettus was famous for its honey. Both Strabo and Pausanias mention it – so there must have been flowers from which the bees could gather it. But the phrase 'violet-crowned' used by Pinder to describe the city of Athens, is more likely to have been inspired by the glow sometimes to be seen as the setting sun strikes the purple of marble slopes, than to be a reference to the flower.

Centuries before, in the days of the Mycenaeans, palaces were being built; the ruins and ground plans can still be traced, but there are no traces of gardens, that most ephemeral of all art forms.

Even today, Greece is not a country famous for domestic horticulture. Lack of space, poor soil and, above all, shortage of water, have never encouraged the cultivation of anything except vines and vegetables. 'The gardens of Adonis', as Shakespeare wrote, 'which one day bloomed, and fruitful were the next', were gardens, if gardens they could be called, of another sort. At a Midsummer Festival, when priests sang laments and dirges for Aphrodite's lover, who had been killed by a wild boar, the statue of the beautiful Adonis was surrounded by pots of plants such as lettuces

Left A visiting yacht anchored in the bay below a green and luxuriantly bordered terrace of Lambros Eftaxias's garden. *Opposite* An antique statue of a Greek youth is the *genius loci* of a terrace with an unrivalled view of the sea, framed in a graceful arch curtained with vines and climbing plants.

and fennel chosen specially for their short lived quality, thus symbolising the short life of the famous Greek youth.

So, with gardens in Greece so rare, it is a special pleasure to come on the cool green terraces created by Lambros Eftaxias, one-time politician and still a famous philanthropist. He has given one of his houses in the Greek capital to the State; this now houses the Museum of Athens to which he has also donated some of its most precious contents.

The garden we show on these pages is at Eleusis, and was created out of unpromising material, 'just rocks and sand – a desert'.

But there were beautiful views of the azure Aegean. Water was brought from Athens, a formidable undertaking, and to this day the garden has to be constantly watered in summer. But with that refreshment, it remains green and bright with flowers all year.

Above left In a country where there is, in summer, a perpetual shortage of water a lawn as verdant and meticulously cut as this is a rarity indeed. In it are paving stones for easy walking, set flush with the turf to make mowing easy. Thanks to regular watering, bright flowers bordering the grass flourish. *Below left* A classical Greek fountain of marble in the form of an antique tablet is set against a rough stone wall – a pleasing contrast of textures. In the foreground another rarity in any Greek garden, a lily pond. Waterlilies like to grow in water that is still. They do not like a fountain's spray to fall on their leaves or flowers – nor do they like to be rocked about. *Opposite above* Leading to an arched and discreetly gated entrance is a path with paving stones spaced out so as to allow for planting between them, as Francis Bacon advised in his essay 'Of Gardens', suggesting plants which do not mind being walked on, but 'which perfume the air most delightfully being trodden upon.' He suggests burnet and thyme, which, like marjoram and mint, all grow wild on the rocky Greek hillsides. 'Therefor you are to set whole alleys of them, to have the pleasure when you walk or tread.' *Below left* Morning Glories (*Ipomaea*) open their azure trumpets to the radiant Greek sunshine. *Below right* Reliable performer in almost every Mediterranean garden – bougainvillea, called after the French eighteenth-century explorer, de Bougainville.

FRANCE

A style invented in the 17th century which made garden history

France can rightly claim the distinction of having, a few miles from its capital, the most famous garden in the world – Versailles. The most famous but, to my mind at least, not the most beautiful. That King of gardeners, and gardener to Kings, André Le Nôtre, created for Louis XIV a garden of the utmost majesty – the last word in 'gardens of the intellect', as they came to be called, that is, gardens planned on the drawing board, with little regard for the existing features of the site. The little hill to the west of the charming stream? It did not fit in with the grand overall plan, so away with it, and 500 French workmen worked away with spades and wheelbarrows to effect its disappearance. If they were not equal to the task, Swiss mercenary soldiers serving in the vicinity were called in to help. The willow-edged stream, too, disappeared, and its waters were used to feed the great canals which crossed and re-crossed Le Nôtre's gigantic design. In short, Nature was first ignored, and then subdued. A thriving village, Choisy-aux-Boeufs, was levelled to the ground. The Great Plan was paramount.

How unlike our own landscape architect, Capability Brown, whose nickname summed up his first concept of garden design: 'Let us consider the capabilities of the site' was his favourite comment on first being shown an area of ground, which it was wished to develop. The great 'Capability' would have cherished the little hill, surmounting it, perhaps, with a simple temple. The stream banks would probably have been tidied up, and a decorative bridge, perhaps in the Chinese style, might have been added.

The French idea was quite different: from the terrace of the Château, whatever its size, avenues of neatly clipped trees radiated towards the horizon. Where two canals crossed, a monumental fountain by Coysevox or Dugoulon would throw their jets over groups of bronze water nymphs dallying in a thicket of bronze bulrushes. Among avenues of trees allowed to reach their natural height, statues of the gods would be placed, in line, between each tree. Deities no longer, but footmen, servants of the King of France. Symmetry, order and proposition were all important, and the famous lawn, Le Tapis Vert, must be the most perfectly proportioned lawn in Europe.

The gardens at Versailles and their forerunner, Vaux Le Vicomte, are André Le Nôtre's masterpieces, but they are masterpieces of architecture, rather than of horticulture. There was, in Le Nôtre's designs no place, as there was to be in English gardens half a century later, for romance or mystery. All was laid down according to rule. One instance: no planting of trees or flowerbeds was to be made in the area cut by the shadow of the château. No ivy and certainly no Virginia creeper, and quite rightly, as they would have looked ridiculous.

However, the renown of the classical French garden is secure It is exemplified in the picture of the garden at the Château de Champs (*opposite*). French gardens have been copied all over Europe, and even in the

Opposite A classical parterre, bright with flowers and sculpture in silvery stone at the Château de Champs, where the garden was enlarged and beautified by Madame de Pompadour in the mid-eighteenth century.

USA and Soviet Union. The garden of the smallest *gentilhommière* still aspires to half an acre of garden in the Versailles style: and formal parterres and regimented lines are still the rule in a hundred municipal pleasuregrounds.

Recently, however, there has been a change; in the past half century, the French have taken to pronouncing their own word *jardinage* with a different, and more English, accent. Trees no longer have to be set in rigid ranks and *allées*. Architecture can be softened by informal planting and flowers. Shrubs, which Le Nôtre would not have countenanced, or indeed even known, are widely planted. The phrase 'herbaceous border' is current in the new language of Franglais, as is the word 'groundcover', with the 'r' rolled in true Gallic fashion.

I have taken care to include some descriptions and pictures of French gardens in the new style, alongside the grandeurs of the past. These smaller gardens are perhaps more to English and American taste. As Harold Nicolson wrote in his introduction to one of my first books, 'a garden is intended for the pleasure of its owner not for ostentation. No one who really cares for flowers can want them arranged in patterns as if they were carpets from Shiraz or Ispahan. Most prefer the shade of some dear familiar tree to the opulence of a parterre displaying its pattern to the wide-open sky. How infinitely preferable to the vast carpets unrolled in front of Versailles.' Harold Nicolson of course was right, though perhaps he over simplified. Madame de Scudéry said of Louis XIV's gardens: '*On les admire, mais on ne les visite pas.*' Nonetheless, His Solar Majesty's gardens are still visited and admired by hundreds of thousands of visitors a year. Whatever the changing fashion, they are still the most famous gardens in the world.

Left In the garden of the Château of Miromesnil in Normandy, home of the Comte and Comtesse de Voguë, there is this beautiful old wall, with simulated windows in rosy brick and silver stone with a cloud of spring blossom above. *Opposite* French gardens are now not always modelled on Versailles. Here, at Le Bois de Moutiers, also in Normandy, home of Monsieur and Madame Mallet, rhododendrons and azaleas show their spring flowers in the light shade and shelter of a wood.

A connoisseur's two gardens in the North and South of France

The Vicomte Charles de Noailles was surely the premier gardener of France, and also vice-president of the British Royal Horticultural Society. He owned two beautiful gardens in France, one at the Villa Pompadour near Paris – shown on the next three pages – and another in the South of France, at Grasse (see page 125). Some years before he died, he was interviewed by Pierre Schneider.

'Surprises are a necessity, even in small gardens and most gardens today tend to be that . . . the stroller must pass from narrow to wide, from dark to light, and so on. A garden that you can see as a whole from the windows of the house, is not a real garden: it holds no surprises . . .'

The Vicomte liked a definite plan of

hedges and paths, 'but within that framework, I like the plants to grow freely – as they please. Over there, for instance, the rugosas spill over the grey border. Why not? If a flower wants to hop over a hedge, let it.

'Statues are an excellent thing in a garden, they are halfway between man and matter – a perfect intermediary between nature and humanity.'

He did not exactly admit to not liking flowers, but said they had to be used with discretion. 'There are flowers for the garden, and flowers for the vases in one's house. They have little in common …' Colour? Too much of it in a garden 'is the sign of a beginner'.

The Vicomte loved plants with grey or silver foliage. 'If you have two colours which are too violent, put something grey between them, to restore the tranquillity.

'There is nothing more pernicious … than the fashion for that red tree called *Prunus pissardii* after a certain M. Pissard, who was a French cook, I believe. Associated with *Acer Negundo* which has white leaves, it makes for the most banal, not to say vulgar combination. Nature never produced a chequerboard.'

'If you eliminate colours, aren't you afraid of falling prey to what you dread most: monotony?' asked his interviewer.

'There are many things more interesting to play with than brutal contrasts of colour. Light and shade, for instance. Look at these paths through the lawn. Instead of using those uncomfortable pebbles you find in so many châteaux, I have employed the grass itself. I am sure Louis XIV would have done the same, had the lawnmower existed. As it was, in those days, cutting the grass with a blade was a costly operation, that had frequently to be repeated. Here, the same grass makes up both the lawn and alleys; but on the latter it is very short, whereas on the former, it is allowed to grow freely. A true gardener is a sculptor as much as a painter. Anyway, the real painter, the real colourist, is not he who relies on colours that are considered beautiful.'

'But surely,' the Vicomte was asked, 'If one were to carry this principle to its logical conclusion, one would make

Opposite top Different greens. 'A hedge need not be flat.' *Below (left to right)* White phlox, red waterlilies, Oriental-looking lotus leaves and pale blue delphiniums. *Above* Lucent foliage, dark evergreens. *Below* A flowery path leads to a leafy corner for conversation.

gardens without any colour, that is without flowers, whatsoever?'

'The Japanese have done so. We Europeans, I confess, haven't yet reached that degree of sophistication.'

Charles de Noailles loved the sound of fountains – not only their appearance. He even liked what he called 'chatty trees', and quoted a friend who once planted a group of aspens near his house 'because they whisper, even when no wind is blowing'.

When asked if he made any distinction between 'noble' and 'common' species, he replied 'what counts is the ensemble, the effect. There is no reason for not mixing flowers and vegetables. That is how it was in the Middle Ages, and that is how it has continued to be in modest gardens. It was the Second Empire, with its heavy-handed luxury, that introduced prejudice by decreeing that vegetables should be hidden from sight. Yet some are very beautiful. I see no reason to hide my corn, and I find certain curly cabbages so handsome that I have used them in my borders. They are halfway between vegetable and flower.'

Beauty is incompatible with laziness of spirit; it is not given but created. 'A bad garden reflects its proprietor's wealth; a good one, his personality', said Monsieur de Noailles. When I see a full-grown olive tree being transported by truck, I know the man who bought it is probably rich, but certainly not a real gardener.

One last point, but one that Charles de Noailles obviously felt strongly about: 'A really devoted gardener must be at home when his flowers are flowering. Plants don't forgive you if you are not present when they are going through the labour of breaking into blossom.'

Above left Light and shade, and an *allée* of Irish yews. *Below left* Friends of the host, relaxing or at work, in the garden of the Villa Pompadour.

The Vicomte de Noailles's garden near Grasse

The Vicomte de Noailles, besides his garden at the Pavillon Pompadour in the North, had another garden in the South of France, at Grasse, the very name of which conjures a faint perfume of its own. Flower scent fascinated Charles de Noailles, but he had strong ideas about it. 'Scent should not cloy, it should come and go, and be an enchanting but short experience.'

Above left A pyramid in silver stone, miniature of the pyramid of Cestius in the Protestant Cemetery in Rome. *Above right* 'In the time of Louis XIV the flower most admired was the peony.' Behind rises another miniature – of one of the fountain pillars at the Villa Aldobrandini near Rome (see also p. 104). *Right* A circular pool set around with pots of arum lilies. Arum lilies will also grow actually in water, where their roots are protected from frost.

Giverny – Home of the painter Claude Monet where he created a legendary garden of waterlilies

Claude Monet first came to live at Giverny just over a century ago: and it was there that he painted his celebrated panels of waterlilies, *Décorations des Nymphéas*. In 1895, he made a water garden in which to grow his beloved waterlilies, spanning the water with a Japanese bridge, hung with early mauve wisteria, followed by white.

It has been said that, of all flowers, waterlilies have a special message for us, but they would have been unable to pass it on to us without the art of Monet. They were his special inspiration, and he would sit for hours among the high grass and sweetly scented cow parsley at the water's edge, his back to the blaze of the flower garden, the Clos Normand, with his eyes fixed on the reflections of the clouds and sky between the waterlilies' flowers. It was there that his work was done. The great Georges Clemenceau, a devoted friend, would say that 'the garden was his studio'.

In 1926, Monet died, and the garden fell into neglect; until 1977, when the distinguished Gerald van der Kemp, Membre de l'Institut, who, with the close co-operation of his wife Florence, had done

such inspired work while in charge of the Palace of Versailles, undertook the preservation of the garden at Giverny. Monsieur and Madame van der Kemp approached their new commitment with dedication and love. The Japanese bridge was replaced, and more waterlilies (some from England) were planted; the flower garden, the Clos Normand, was converted from a neglected and unloved area, into a scene of joyous exuberance, with roses, lilacs, peonies, poppies and all the gayest flowers of summer, playing their part in what Vita Sackville-West described to me once as a 'rumpus of colour'. Roses with names like *Cuisse de Nymphe émue* – 'thigh of a startled nymph' – and a peony called *Belle Duchesse*. Odd how things sound more glamorous in French.

But whenever one thinks of Giverny, one thinks of waterlilies, the flowers to which, if flowers can be immortal, Monet gave immortality. Clemenceau quotes him as saying, 'I only looked at what the universe showed me, to bear witness to it with my paintbrush. Surely this is something.' Something indeed.

Below Waterlilies, with their round green leaf-pads float amid the reflections of surrounding trees. *Opposite above left* Weeping willows, in Latin *Salix*, in French so beautifully *Pleureuses*, by the water's brink. *Above right* In the Clos Normand. Spring blossom and narcissus on a close shorn lawn, with Monet's house beyond. *Below left* The mauve sprays of wisteria and the delicate pink of an azalea make the very picture of spring. *Below right* The restored and repainted Japanese bridge, festooned with flower.

Un Jardin Franglais

Baroness de Waldner, until a few years ago the occupant of La Grange, describes the garden she made there: 'It was French – but with English feelings'. Madame de Waldner now lives in Provence where, in spite of a rather different climate, she is creating another beautiful garden. La Grange is a property of the Duc de Gramont.

'La Grange was once Pauline Borghese's farmhouse, and it is where she used to have her famous milk baths, while staying with her brother King Joseph Bonaparte at his nearby Château de Mortefontaine. The garden in Pauline's time must have looked very French, with terraces, water, islands and a fine pigeon house.

'Now, it is without any special nationality; just a garden that has been loved by me, my family and my friends. Like all beginners, at first I was tempted to grow shrubs and trees that, as I learnt afterwards, insisted on acid soil. But after a few setbacks, and some disappointments, I concentrated on transforming the soil (grey powdery sand) into good rich earth, fed with horse and cow manure; naturally, I made my own compost, without which no gardener can ever achieve any form of success. I planted climbing roses, and a yew hedge, which I fed with blood transfusions from the local butcher.

'Twelve squares were drawn out, and surrounded by lavender "Hidcote Blue", which is the one I prefer, though it is difficult to find in France. Six squares of vegetables, six squares of flowers. I was drawn towards a herbaceous border, of course, but I soon realized that each country must in principle stick to its own speciality. Thanks to frequent visits to the Chelsea Flower Show, I started the garden like most people furnish a house. Small plants, such as *Cupressus elwoodii*, lots of saxifrages and sempervivums regularly crossed the Channel, hidden in my husband's shirts, or my best Ascot clothes.

'The highlight of my early planting career was a *Magnolia grandiflora* which flowered when I was away, and died of a chill the following winter. I planted few large trees as, alas, I was not the owner of that paradise, only the tenant.

'After fifteen years of hard work, with a gardener who got too old to be at my beck and call, Edouard came into my life. He

Opposite Four views of the garden at La Grange. *Right* Beyond the flower-filled garden lies the lake of Mortefontaine.

was a great character: a jolly solid Flemish type, like a Franz Hals, and, besides gardening, was a wonderful cook and made the best mayonnaise I have ever tasted. In the garden, he specialized in vegetables and dahlias. Within one year, my front garden was turned into a doll's house garden, with all the green vegetables transferred to a new kitchen garden, which Edouard created down by the river. Edouard belonged to the old school (I do not wish to insult the young) but he worked on his own, without any help, from dawn to dusk in two gardens and two greenhouses. He sailed up and down the drive, over the road, and back again on a bright red tractor, humming and beaming with joy. He and I aspired to eucryphias and *Lapageria rosea* (called after Pauline's sister-in-law, the Empress Josephine, née La Pagerie, whom she disliked so much). Sweet-scented geraniums, such as "Mabel Grey" and *tomentosum* from England, were favourites, as well as marvellous pelargoniums, "acquired" from English and Scottish greenhouses.'

Baroness de Waldner has a special feeling for plants. She will rhapsodize over a black pansy she saw at Hatfield, and not rest until she has acquired a root; and in her garden in Paris she managed to carve an elephant out of privet bushes.

Above The garden of La Grange offered every delight of summer, with flower colour everywhere, the scent of roses and the cool gleam of water. English touches were the pergola arch, and the massed groups of simple flowers.

Gardens in the north, the south and in Paris

Above Two views of Bois de Moutiers in Normandy, where the château was built by the English architect Sir Edwin Lutyens, and the garden is said to have been planned under the influence of the great Gertrude Jekyll. The grey stone façade of the château, with its mullioned windows, is wreathed with the flowers of *Clematis montana* and, as can be seen in both pictures, the formally laid out garden, with its yew hedges, paved paths and symmetrical flowerbeds, is planted with white tulips. 'We do believe', says Madame Mallet, 'that Miss Jekyll, by letter, gave precious advice.' *Below* The French have a genius for turning gardens into drawing rooms, unlike the Anglo-Saxons who are more inclined to turn drawing rooms into gardens. To the left, geraniums, generously massed, to dress a wall of a terrace garden in the South of France, and to the right white petunias on an elegant ball-capped 'dresser' in a niche in a garden in Paris. To the right, white geraniums and that favourite of town garden designers, a clipped bay tree.

BELGIUM

The Château d'Annevoie takes full advantage of an untiring water supply

Belgium has many beautiful gardens, but my favourite and the one I seem to know the best, is the garden which the present happy owner, Monsieur de Montpellier d'Annevoie, has, with the aid of his ancestor Charles-Alexis de Montpellier, and 200 years of development, created at the Château d'Annevoie in the valley of the Meuse near Namur.

The original layout of the gardens was planned about 1750, and ever since, successive members of the family have embellished it. But credit for the first, inspired, plan must go to Charles-Alexis: and in devising his great pleasureground he had an important natural ally – a never failing water supply – and the imagination to make the very most of it. In his erudite and succinct notes on his garden, Monsieur de Montpellier d'Annevoie – of the twelfth generation of his family to live in Belgium, has written: 'Annevoie's greatest original feature is water ... you will see it in many places – fountains, cascades ... a real aquatic landscape: which is, moreover, a natural phenomenon: not one machine or pump behind this magic. Charles-Alexis simply put to use four abundant sources in the forest. He canalized the waters and took advantage of the uneven aspect of the grounds to play the fountains. Artificial reservoirs collected the waters, and both the lie of the landscape and the pressure led to these aquatic beauty spots, where for more than two hundred years, fountains have been sparkling gaily, in winter as in summer.'

Below A broad walk leading to the Château, brightened by gay parterres.
Opposite The Allée des Fleurs in a garden which shows signs of Anglo-Saxon influence with its multi-coloured flowerbeds.

Opposite above left The 'Little Canal' seen from an airy bridge with web-like hand-rails. The visitor to the garden has to pause every so often during his tour to admire the imagination and taste evinced in every detail, architectural or horticultural, by the garden's creators.
Above right Les Nappes d'Eau, another difficult phrase to translate. Let us settle for cascade – a cascade falling over regularly cut steps. That great expert on gardens, Sir George Sitwell, once wrote, in *On the Making of Gardens*, that water flowing over a stepped cascade made a quite different noise from that supplied by the 'shifting curves of a fountain', and aptly described it as 'deep-toned music'.
Below The 'Water Buffet'. The lavish use of water to decorate the garden at Annevoie must surely be unique, and is thanks entirely to Nature's bounty. M. Pechère, President of the International Committee of Historic Gardens, has written these words about the use of water at Annevoie: 'It cannot be equalled by any other gardens, not even Versailles itself, where the fountains may only be admired on rare occasions. At Annevoie, they flow forever . . .'
Above right One of the most striking fountains in the garden, its rising jets making a mound of sparkling water, is called *Le Grand Bouillon* – difficult to translate into English – the 'Big Bubble' perhaps – though that is hardly an elegant enough name for anything at Annevoie.
Above left At the junction of several avenues is the 'Pond of the Round-Point', a miniature piece of water, with another fountain, eight spidery sprays rising and falling against the dark greenery beyond.
Below A sculpture of Mercury after the chisel of Giovanni da Bologna (1524–1608) in an arched arbour of greenery.

HOLLAND

An untypical garden recently restored in the land of tulips

When one thinks of gardens in Holland, one thinks of tulips – and with good reason – but the splendid garden of the Paleis Het Loo, shown opposite, is totally, one might almost say, triumphantly, un-Dutch in feeling. In the last few years, both the palace and the garden have been brilliantly restored to how they looked when built and laid out by Stadtholder William, afterwards William III of England, very much in the favoured style of his worst enemy, Louis XIV. The rehabilitation of Paleis Het Loo shows the greatest good taste and imagination, and its restorers and the Dutch people are to be congratulated on their achievement.

However, Holland will always be thought of as the land of tulips, and the finest collection, not only of tulips, but of all plants grown from bulbs, is to be found at the Keukenhof garden. Before describing in detail this great garden, a few words about the history of the tulip itself.

Tulips are comparative newcomers to the Western world. It is doubtful if Queen Elizabeth I ever saw one. The famous herbalist John Gerard, describes the tulip in 1597 as 'a strange and forrein flower' which had lately arrived in England by way of Vienna, from Turkey, the native land of many species of tulip. In passing, I should mention that the word tulip comes from the Turkish *dulband*, a turban, which the flowers of the first tulips were thought to resemble.

If little was known about tulips in 1600 they became too well known in Holland, at least twenty or so years later, when Tulipomania – or a craze for rare and cross-bred tulips – hit the usually so level-headed Dutch. Rare bulbs would be sold for small fortunes or if not for ready cash, exchanged for thoroughbred horses or farms. *Tulpenwoede* (*woede* is the Dutch word for fury) lasted only a few years, and is well described in Alexandre Dumas's famous novel *The Black Tulip*. By 1637 the fury had passed, and the Dutch came to their senses once more.

But back to our own times, and to the Keukenhof, where you will find every sort, size and shape of tulip, though, on my many visits, I do not remember a truly black one.

Keukenhof lies between the two great modern roads that link The Hague and Haarlem, near the village of Lisse. A few miles only from the coast, it is sheltered from the winds of the North Sea by high sand-dunes. The story of how the garden came into being is a short one. In 1949, when the estate of Keukenhof, for years the country seat of the distinguished family of Van Lynden, had become, owing to changing conditions, difficult to maintain, the enterprising bulb-growers of Holland saw a magnificent opportunity of putting into effect a long cherished idea. By the

Opposite The Paleis Het Loo and its splendid formal garden, richly patterned in flowers and coloured gravel, have recently been lavishly restored. They now look as they did in the late seventeenth century when built and laid out by the Stadtholder William, later King William III of England.

spring of 1950 over fifty acres of the neglected woodland had been cleared. Dead trees were removed; marshes were turned into lawns; ditches were filled in; ugly patches were remodelled; stagnant ponds were conjured into lucent pools and other amenities were added to make the garden the delight of the million people who visit it every year.

Every spring the garden is bright with sapphire-blue muscari, the gold of daffodils and, of course, tulips in colours 'to make the rash gazer wipe his eye' – tulips in scarlet uniform, and of as erect stance as any London guardsman, or striped like a troubadour's hose. The 'strange and forrein flower' has certainly come a long way since Gerard's day.

But before we leave the garden at Keukenhof, we must just mention the hyacinths, in their softer, subtler colours, seducing the eye and laying their fragrance (which most tulips lack) on the air around them.

Recently a new part of the garden at Keukenhof has been developed, and borders of flowers for later in the season, planted. A canal has been cut, and an impressive range of fountains set in place.

Above In the world-famous Keukenhof garden, flower-laden branches of a Japanese cherry tree canopy a drift of tulips. *Opposite above left* A group of perfectly grown striped tulips take and hold the eye. 'Clusiana', 'Princeps' and 'Artist' are three of the best particoloured ones. *Above right* A long narrow parterre in full flower contrasts with the still bare branches of early spring. *Centre left* One of the sights of the Keukenhof garden early in the season is this long swathe of scillas and muscari (grape hyacinths) their brilliant blue a reproach to the grey Dutch sky above. *Below* the light soil and high water-table of the garden provide ideal conditions for growing bulbs.

GERMANY

Where the grandest gardens were conjured in the 18th century and beautiful roses in the 19th

The Countess von Arnim, in her famous book about an Englishwoman's horticultural experiences in the Fatherland, *Elizabeth and her German Garden*, gives amusing descriptions of her efforts, which, being a novice, were not always successful.

'I sent to England for vegetable-marrow seeds, as they are not grown here, and people try and make boiled cucumbers take their place; but boiled cucumbers are nasty things, and I don't see why marrows should not do perfectly well. These, and primrose-roots, are the English contributions to my garden. I brought over the roots in a tin box last time I came from England, and am anxious to see whether they will consent to live here. Certain it is that they don't exist in the Fatherland, so I can only conclude the winter kills them, for surely, if such lovely things would grow, they never would have been overlooked ... But they are not going to do anything this year, and I only hope those cold days did not send them off to the Paradise of flowers. I am afraid their first impression of Germany was a chilly one.'

Primroses are exquisitely beautiful, the much-loved harbingers of spring, with a very special character of their own. Everyone loves and welcomes them, in spite of Wordsworth's non-hero, the dullard Peter Bell, for whom

> A primrose by a river's brim
> A yellow primrose was to him
> and it was nothing more.

And besides the promise they bring, and their frail-seeming beauty, they have a constitution as tough as old boots. I have seen carpets of them on the 'brim' of Lake Mainau (page 145) – of primroses, and of their cousins, cowslips.

Germany has almost as good a climate for gardening as anywhere, although the passion for domestic gardening is, perhaps, not so inborn as it is elsewhere. Professional gardeners, and botanists Germany has never lacked. Did not Leonard Fuchs (1501–66) give his name to the fuchsia, Johann Deutz (1743–88) to the deutzia and Christian Weigel (1748–1831) to the weigela?

And German rose breeders and hybridizers – for example W. Kordes, to mention but one – are unrivalled in Europe. 'Frühlingsduft' (breath of spring), 'Frühlingsgold' (spring gold) and 'Frühlingsmorgen' (spring morning) are all German roses with beautiful flowers, and beautiful names

Opposite The magnificent Residenz of Würzburg was built by the great Balthasar Neumann about 1720. The garden was created some years later by Prince Bishop Adam von Seinsheim, and is a splendid example of the German rococo style.

to go with them. 'Raubritter', another rose raised by Kordes, is one of the most delicious of all fairly modern roses, with its pink flowers which look as if they were made of shells; it burst on a delighted world in 1936 (see page 146). It is sad that such a lovely creation should have such an unattractive name; though another very handsome German rose, with flowers of unfading crimson and a heroic constitution, has the least alluring name of them all – 'Parkdirektor Riggers'. I hope that the good Herr Parkdirektor will forgive me for saying so. So much for modern German garden skills.

It was in the eighteenth century that gardens in Germany really first flourished. Frederick the Great created at Sans-Souci a garden entirely terraced in greenhouses, for he had exotic tastes; tuberoses were grown and other plants from the tropics, such as brunfelsia, which flowers in three different shades of blue at once – that was also called after a German botanist.

Under Frederick's influence French taste was paramount all over the princely states of Germany. Versions of Versailles, with gardens to match, sprang up everywhere. One of the most typical and best laid out, an example of formal German gardening at its best, is at Brühl, outside Cologne – pictured here.

Flower brilliance in the baroque garden of Augustusberg Schloss at Brühl

The many princelings and dukelings of the Holy Roman Empire – which Voltaire held was neither Holy, Roman nor an Empire – were great builders: some were great gardeners, too. If they are remembered at all today, it is for their 'policies' (pleasuregrounds, in the Scottish sense), rather than for their policies. Such a ruler was the Elector Palatine of Bavaria, who created the magical garden at Schwetzingen near Mannheim with its lilacs and stag-headed fountains. So, too, was the Prince Bishop of Würzburg, who conjured the Veitshochheim garden.

The creator of the beautiful setting of the Augustusberg Schloss at Brühl, near Bonn, was another such princely gardener, and it was the Elector Clemens August of Cologne who laid the plans of the garden which the visitor to Brühl admires today. An early design (about 1728) was by the Frenchman Dominique Girard, a pupil of Le Nôtre, and though altered and adapted over the years, it survives today, and shows the influence of Le Nôtre's stupendous creation at Versailles; but it is on a far smaller scale.

Left Symmetrically clipped bay trees in *Caissons de Versailles* – the influence of Versailles is everywhere apparent at Brühl. *Above* A stone urn enriched with gilding. *Opposite above* A balustraded terrace and stair leads from the castle to a flower-carpeted garden, with elaborate *broderies* of box enlivened with flower colour. *Below left* Palm trees in movable boxes stand outside the orangery in summer. *Below right* A miniature parterre which is in perfect proportion to a cream painted *Gartenhaus*.

Schloss Mainau and its garden on the banks of Lake Constance

It has been said that in Lake Constance on the southern borders of Germany there is an island which is all garden, for on it, Prince Bernadotte, a cousin of the King of Sweden, has planned and planted a splendid pleasureground.

Early in the last century, the then owner of the Island of Mainau was the Grand Duke of Baden who, in the sentimental fashion of the time, asked dear friends to plant trees which afterwards were neatly labelled; he also had rocks carved with lines from the more famous German poets. His great grandson has respected his forebear's taste, but has added life and vigour to the garden by generous planting in today's style, with carpets of massed tulips and the newest discoveries in the world of trees. For instance, there is an avenue of trees, *Metasequoia glyptostroboides*, a species only rediscovered just after the Second World War, in a distant province of China. Giant sequoias were imported from the West Coast of America and gingkos, another tree which for centuries was thought no longer to exist, were planted. The gingko, said to be a very distant relation of the yew, has fern-like leaves which are quite distinct from those of any other tree; hence its popular name, the Maidenhair Tree.

Opposite From a carpet of spring flowers, and framed in the young foliage of tall trees, rises the tower of the Chapel at Schloss Mainau. *Above and below* Rich plantings of tulips on a tree-bordered bank, and (*below*) a formal gravel path.

Glimpses of German gardens

Above The spreading layout of the garden of the Charlottenburg Palace in Berlin. The garden, showing strong French influence, was planned for Frederick Wilhelm (1688–1740), the first King of Prussia, 'who first found, in palaces and gardens, an ample field for his love of magnificence'. Frederick Wilhelm was the father of Frederick the Great. The

garden, owing to its abundant water supply, is rich in fountains and canals: it lies on the banks of the river Spree. *Below left* Tree peonies in the garden of the Palace at Würzburg. *Below right* One of the best of all roses raised in Germany, with shell-like pink flowers, and a very ugly name, 'Raubritter'. It was a product of the famous firm of W. Kordes.

Opposite At Bad Driburg in Westphalia, the *Gräfliches Haus*, home of Count and Countess von Oeynhausen, is surrounded by a beautiful garden. *Below right* An unusual fan-shaped bridge spans a stream, in a late summer setting of flowers, shrubs and weeping willow. *Above* An elegantly painted *Caisson de Versailles* planted with attractive

originality. Glistening dark green holly and red-berried cotoneaster make a particoloured obelisk. *Above right* With the house walls curtained in autumnal scarlet, a broad paved terrace leads towards a white painted seat in the Chinese Chippendale style. *Below* An eighteenth-century pavilion with classical pediment.

RUSSIA

Gilded magnificence in the harshest of climates

St Petersburg had been founded in 1703 on the most unpromising site imaginable, near where the river Neva – whose very name, in Finnish, means mud – emptied its brown waters into the Baltic. But what Peter the Great wanted above all else, was an outlet to the sea – a doorway to civilized Europe. In building the new capital of Russia, hundreds of thousands may have died, but, through the Tsar's iron will, drive and pertinacity, the end was achieved, and one of the great cities of the world rose in splendour. By 1716, the capital was well on the way to completion and Peter, while on his travels in Germany had met, and made friends with, a young Frenchman – he was in his early thirties – Alexandre Jean Baptiste Le Blond. Le Blond had worked with the great Le Nôtre at Versailles, and when, after the death of Louis XIV in 1715, much of the work at Versailles came to an end, Le Blond, like many other French architects and artists at that time, looked abroad for fresh fields in which to exercise his talents – garden design was his special study; he had, in his own rather complacent words, already planted 'several fine gardens'.

With the offer of a handsome salary, 5,000 roubles a year, and a high-sounding title, 'Architect General of St Petersburg', Le Blond made his way to Russia, then regarded, with some reason, as being on the very fringe of the civilized world. Soon he was well established in what came to be called the Palmyra of the North, where he laid out the capital's most famous street, the Nevsky Prospect. Then he was asked to advise on the choice of a site for a country palace, where there were the 'capabilities', as the English garden designer Lancelot Brown might have called them, of creating a fabulous garden.

The site that the Tsar and Le Blond finally settled on was far more promising than the one upon which St Petersburg had, with such difficulty, been built. About twenty miles outside the new city they found a sharply rising ridge simply asking to be crowned with a noble building. From the windows of the palace-to-be, Peter would be able to watch his finest new toy of all, his new navy, spread its sails on the gulf of Finland. Perfect. Peter took the closest interest in all the plans, and some of his own sketches survive.

Thousands of trees were planted to clothe the chilly slopes round Peterhof, as the palace was to be called – mostly firs, maples and elms, which were native to Russia, but many, too, which were exotics in Muscovy, such as limes, beeches and different fruit trees. Some, at least, took root and lived. As I wrote over twenty years ago: '. . . in spite of cold, two hundred endless Russian winters, and the ravages of the last war, many trees of the first planting are still there, and the park at Peterhof today presents a picture of smiling verdure'.

Most striking of all the features of the garden at Peterhof must surely be the fountains and cascades in front of the palace itself. Foaming water flows on either side of a grotto, tumbles down lofty marble steps, over gilded

Above Samson and the lion, commemorating the victory at Poltava. *Opposite* When the fountains play, water falls down lofty marble steps, over gilded risers.

risers, and between two serried rows of statues and classical urns, also gilded. It then fills a great semicircular pool, with more golden sculptures crowning rocky pedestals, and overflows into the noblest of several canals which run, like radiating avenues of water, towards the sea.

The dominating sculpture at the base of the cascade deserves special mention. It shows Samson in mortal combat with a lion, from whose jaws a powerful column of water rises. It commemorates Peter the Great's most famous victory – over the invading Swedes at Poltava, in 1709.

Two other water-features in the garden are more light-hearted. In one pool, with water spraying in every direction, an artificial dog pursues artificial ducks round and round, uttering dog- and duck-like noises. In another corner of the garden, there is a life-like, but man-made, oak tree, which, at the turning of a secret tap, sprays water over anyone standing near, a device which must have appealed to Peter's boisterous sense of humour.

Wherever the ground is flat at Peterhof, there are bright beds of flowers, their colours caught and reflected by the fountains' jets. The water for these comes from springs in the nearby Ropsha Hills, and has a specially luminous sparkle.

The garden at Peterhof could only have been conjured in Russia. For the Western visitor, perhaps, there is too much gilding, too many different coloured marbles, too much garish bedding-out – particularly when the sun is shining. But in Russia, the sun often does not shine, and it is then that there is something brave and heartening, under threatening grey skies, in all the glitter and the gold.

Opposite A broad canal runs towards the sea. *Above* The 'Hothouse fountain' throws up a single slender jet. *Below* One of Peter's water toys. A dog pursues ducks, all uttering appropriate noises.

SCANDINAVIA

A son of Scandinavia achieved world fame in botany

One hardly thinks of the three beautiful countries that comprise Scandinavia as countries famous for their gardens. And yet, with their short summers, perhaps flowers are more prized in those Northern lands than in countries with gentler climates; botany has always been a favourite study in Scandinavia. Denmark produced a series of porcelain plates, made in Copenhagen's China Factory decorated with the Flora Danica, which made the wild flowers of Denmark famous the world over.

The Danish writer of fairy tales, Hans Andersen, wrote a story 'The Garden of Paradise', which was about plants, though in a somewhat fanciful manner. A prince, it seems, was carried away, in the friendliest fashion, by the 'East Wind', in the form of a Chinese. After a while, they reached a fabulous garden. What a scene met their eyes. There 'flowed a river, as clear as the atmosphere itself: gold and silver fish swam in it: purple eels, which emitted blue sparks . . . were playing below the surface, and the broad leaves of the water lily shone with all the colours of the rainbow: the flowers themselves were like glowing orange coloured flames, receiving sustenance from the water, as a lamp from oil. A bridge of marble, shining like a glassy pearl . . . led over the water to the Island of Bliss, where bloomed the Garden of Paradise.'

The Prince entered the garden and 'the flowers and leaves sang the sweetest songs . . . in soft wavy tones . . . whether they were palm trees or gigantic water plants . . . the Prince knew not.' Such was Hans Andersen's vision of the Garden of Paradise. Very far from the Danish gardens he had probably been brought up in, with their picket fences, sunflowers, yellow daisies, and simple, sweet-scented roses.

Another Andersen story in which plants play an important part is a less well known one, 'Little Ida's Flowers'. Ida was told by her student friend that, when the King of Denmark (after whom the famous geranium was named) left his country palace after his summer holiday, and returned to

Left A thatched cottage and flower–filled garden, perfect setting for a Hans Andersen fairy story. *Opposite* Frijsenborg Slot, a terraced and turreted Danish castle and family home of the distinguished Wedell family.

Copenhagen, all the flowers of his garden hurried into the palace to welcome him. 'The two loveliest roses sat on the thrones (what did the King think of that?) and acted King and Queen. The red cockscombs then arranged themselves in rows before them, and bowed very low. The prettiest of the flowers then came in, and opened the ball. Blue violets represented midshipmen, and danced with the hyacinths and crocus who took the part of young ladies. Tulips and tall orange lilies played the part of old dowagers, whose business it was to see that everything went on with perfect propriety . . .'

But it is Sweden that has contributed one of the greatest of all names to our gardening vocabulary: Carl von Linné (1707–78), known to the world as Linnaeus. It was he, simple son of poor parents in Smöland, who studied botany at the great Swedish university of Uppsala under Celsius in the early eighteenth century, and afterwards gave an inestimable gift to horticulture by fixing for all time the nomenclature of plants as it is recognized today. Without Linnaeus, cyclamen might still be known as Sowbread, and artemisia as Old Man. These are only two out of thousands of examples of plants, which before had been known by their colloquial name, unintelligible outside their country of origin. By giving them Latin names, Linnaeus established a universal botanical vocabulary, a *Who's Who* of plants, so to speak, which is intelligible to Swede, Anglo-Saxon and Japanese alike. No wonder that in his lifetime he was hailed as the Dioscorides Secundus, and Princeps Botanicorum.

A human side to Linnaeus's character must be mentioned, a foible, which links Sweden for ever with the world of botany. To many of his favourite plants he gave the names of his favourite pupils or colleagues. Hence rudbeckia, after Olaf Rudbeck; alstroemeria, after Baron Clas Alstroemer; and kalmia after Peter Kalm.

As for Norway, we do not remember flower pieces painted by Norway's most famous painter Munch, or much mention of Norwegian flowers in Ibsen's plays; but Oslo, Norway's capital, possesses a fine botanic garden as can be seen here.

Above and below Two pictures of the beautiful Botanic Garden in Oslo, founded in 1814. *Opposite above and below left* Though summers in Norway are short, they are filled with flowers. *Bottom right* A lawn on a roof might present mowing problems.

Sculpture in a lakeside garden

The garden at Rottneros was planned in the late 1930s on a site overlooking beautiful Lake Fryken, by Dr Svante Pahison. It covers nearly a hundred acres and is planted with rare trees and rhododendrons. But its unusual quality lies in the fact that it houses some examples of sculpture by famous Swedish sculptors, headed by Carl Milles (1875–1955).

Above In the centre of the circular rose garden and with a Swedish version of the Winged Victory of Samothrace in the distance, stands a statue of Prince Gustav of Sweden in immaculate Victorian frock coat. *Below left* By an informal path, marigolds and claret-coloured love-lies-bleeding make a brightly coloured carpet. *Below right* Carl Milles, the famous

Swedish sculptor, created this fountain over sixty years ago. It is surrounded by four naked maidens in lead, and modelled on his famous Orpheus Fountain in Stockholm. *Above* A decorative pool, with clumps of day lilies and hostas on either side, leads the eye from the King's Garden towards the central lawn, which is kept impeccably mown.

Below left A wide swathe of lawn between bright borders has the Victory of Samothrace, on her lofty pillar, as focal point. *Below right* Low-clipped hedges, with higher walls of greenery on either side, in the classical French style, run towards a distant view of Lake Fryken, which is as blue as the waters of the Mediterranean, though by the Baltic Sea.

SCOTLAND

Flower-filled gardens not only on the favoured West Coast

Why, when gardens in the north of England are certainly less lush than those in the south, are some of the gardens of Scotland so luxuriant? The answer, in three words, is the Gulf Stream, said to account for one fifth of the total heat of the North Atlantic, which, without it, they say might freeze.

But out of the seven beautiful Scottish gardens we show in the next few pages, only two are on the favoured west coast of Scotland – the coast that receives the benefits of the famous Gulf Stream. The others are on, or near, the chilly east coast, and one, the spectacular garden at Drummond Castle, is not near any coast at all, but in the middle of Perthshire. But, certainly, when the castle of Drummond was first founded, in 1491, Scotland was less bonny than she could be described as today.

The heather and the mountains were there, but there were few trees, few flowers, and in a country which was continually at war with England, it is unlikely that there were many gardens. The climate, too, had a strange reputation. Few plants, apparently, could survive it. A visiting Italian prelate, who, brave man, made a tour of Scotland in the reign of King James I (1394–1437), mentions not only the bareness of the countryside, but a very extraordinary pear tree which he was told produced fruit in the shape of geese, which, when ripe, dropped off and flew away. Nor, he reported, were vegetables much grown – and the Scottish despised people who ate them, such as 'the soft Kail-eating Grants'.

Even in the seventeenth century, Fynes Morison wrote: 'In the Northern parts of England they have small pleasantnesse or abundance of fruit and flower, so in Scotland they must have lesse and none at all.'

There is certainly an abundance of flowers in the garden of Drummond Castle of which there are pictures on these and the next two pages.

The garden at Drummond is terraced, like many in Scotland where there are far more terraced gardens surrounding old historic houses than there are in England. The reason is not hard to find. In the early seventeenth century, when the taste for decorative gardening was growing in Scotland, as it was in England, the houses of the great landowners were still fortresses. The times were still too unsettled for country houses like Hatfield, with its smiling façade and 'walls of glass', to be practical. There were still feuds and forays and midnight attacks to contend with, and houses had to be easy to defend.

But times improved, and by Victorian days the garden at Drummond was as elaborately maintained as any in Britain. During the Second World War it fell into neglect and the borders and parterres were all but obliterated with weeds and brambles. The paths, some evergreens, and the statuary survived, but only just. With immense hard work and imagination, the garden has been revived. But in restoring its rich pattern, the late Earl and Countess of Ancaster, father and mother of the present owner Baroness Willoughby de Eresby, used plants altogether in the modern way.

Opposite A spectacular view from the balustraded terrace of Drummond Castle over the resuscitated Victorian garden, with gravel replacing areas which were once extravagantly bedded out. Those conifers and red-leaved Japanese maples that survived the overgrowth of brambles and nettles during the war, have been carefully retained, and give long-lasting colour, while flower colour though more short-lived, is supplied by Hidcote lavender and low hedges in a St Andrew's cross pattern of evergrey anaphalis. As centre point, there is an old Scottish sundial, dated 1630, and designed by John Milne.

Evergreens and everygreys replaced geraniums and calceolarias; and hardy perennial herbaceous plants, such as anaphalis and Miss Jekyll's own lavender, made up the overall design. The garden, triumphantly, came back to life.

Dr Johnson, who was against Scotland generally, described its climate as so bad that the Scots had to grow their crops under glass. How wrong he was. Scotland has gardens as fine as any in the British Isles, and many of the great gardeners in the last 200 years have been Scottish.

By the end of the eighteenth century, Scottish gardeners were well abreast of gardeners south of the border. They were making names for themselves to such an extent that the English were jealous. At that time, the curator of the Chelsea Physic Garden was a Scot, Phillip Miller.

In Victorian times, Scottish gardens and gardeners were as good as any in the United Kingdom, and they 'carpet-bedded' with the best, achieving effects no whit less hideous than their English neighbours.

Opposite above Warm-coloured conifers and deciduous trees with interesting leaves stud a rare area of lawn. *Below* A bust of a Roman worthy views one of the main cross paths of the great parterre at Drummond, hedged on either side with anaphalis showing its starry white flowers. *Above* The old tower surmounted by a flagstaff looks over the terraces to the lower garden. *Below left* An old gateway of carved stone with swags of fruit, flowers and drapery carved in bold relief. *Below right* The main paths are of crisp local gravel.

Keir, in Stirlingshire

Though there must have been some sort of garden at Keir since the fifteenth century (the name Keir means a camp or fort, and the place may once have been the site of a Roman fort), the garden in its present splendid form dates from the late eighteenth century. This was a period of great development and prosperity in Scotland, and the Stirling family, Lairds of Keir for hundreds of years, were progressive landlords and farmers. They were in the forefront of every agricultural enterprise, and the capital that flowed in from their estates in Jamaica, made it possible to rebuild farms, reclaim marshland and plant trees by the thousand: they had the taste and the means to beautify the immediate surroundings of their eighteenth-century house.

A plan, made by Thomas White (born *c.*1736, and a pupil of Capability Brown) in 1801, shows the existing walled garden as it is now, and the Scottish architect David Hamilton (1768–1843), a 'distinguished classicist of his day', had a hand in designing the present terrace. By early in Queen Victoria's reign the gardens must have looked much as they do now.

One remarkable survival, from those different, more spacious days, is the approach road to the back door of the house. This is by the way of a tunnel, hidden below a built-up terrace and a bridge, so that the Laird's eyes should not be offended by a glimpse of a tradesman's cart.

The gardens of Keir are surely some of the most beautiful and best planted in Scotland. The formal area near the house,

Left Steps lead from a flower-filled border.
Above Buttresses of gold and green.

with its lofty sandstone terrace, soaring flights of steps, and immaculately tailored topiary, blends, with no sharp change of mood, into informally planned lawn and woodland walks. All summer the borders, especially those to be seen from the windows of the house, fairly blaze with colour: and the flowers that fill them are not the usual run-of-the-mill herbaceous material, but the best varieties of today – such as the penstemons 'Garnet' and 'Sir Frederick Moore', *Salvia patens* 'Blue Beard', *Nepeta* 'Six Hills Giant', as well as aconitum, eupatorium and bocconia, with its glaucous leaves, like aces of clubs.

Perhaps it is the trees and shrubs of Keir which are the garden's most remarkable feature. Some are of a great age: a Spanish chestnut (*Castanea sativa*) is said to have been planted 450 years ago – soon after the Battle of Flodden – and the tallest dawn redwood (*Metasequoia*) in Scotland is to be found at Keir.

Some of the more unusual trees which are of special interest to connoisseurs include two remarkable nothofagus, planted in the past twenty years, *N. procera* and *N. betuloides*, and that brilliant autumn colourer *Malus tschonoskii*, as well as several stewartias, which flower in late summer when there is little competition from other flowering trees.

Top left A galaxy of dahlias. *Top right* Twin urns frame a perfect lawn. *Above left* The pale gold of autumn leaves. *Above right* An urn-capped column of yew.

Tyninghame in West Lothian

It has been said about the garden at Tyninghame that it seems, more than most other gardens, to be the immediate child of its owners, the creation of their imagination and fancy, an extension and expression of their personality. It is the home of the Earl and Countess of Haddington, and Lady Haddington, a very beautiful but modest woman, would be the first to say that there was a garden at Tyninghame long before she came there. Doubtless there was, but one expects that it was rather conventional. The present occupants have given it a special aura. Unashamedly Victorian, with its turrets and terracotta walls, the house is not beautiful, but it has a romantic, almost fairy-tale look; and the garden is magical.

Inverewe in Ross and Cromarty

Opposite above A luxurious herbaceous border, set close in the modern style, with weed-defeating plants, and an informal edging of cushiony santolina. *Below left* Modern planting trends at their best. Hardy blue agapanthus and pink *Polygonum affine*, flowing happily over a warm gravel path. *Below right* Another modern gardening trend, a froth of white roses climbing up old apple trees.

David Paton, a garden lover and photographer, first saw the garden at Loch Ewe during the Second World War, where 'a motley collection of merchant ships would assemble ... for the perilous convoy to Russia'. The barren mountains, driving wind and rain 'hardly seemed a suitable site for one of the loveliest botanic gardens' he had ever seen.

The garden was first planted in 1862 by Osgood Mackenzie, with visionary audacity. Such was his success, energy and pertinacity that he created a paradise of trees and flowers, for that is what the garden at Inverewe now is. It is a garden which certainly must benefit from the Gulf Stream, for in it now grows a unique collection of subtropical plants. Space only

allows mention of a chosen few. Besides rare rhododendrons, as can be seen in the pictures above, *Narcissus cyclameneus*, *Myosotidium hortensia*, the Chatham Island violet, *Arbutus unedo*, and two very special South Africans – *Agapanthus orientalis* and *Rhodohypoxis baurii*, grow in the garden. David Paton writes of beautiful Inverewe: 'Its splendour does not depend only on numbers, but on their setting, and the skill with which it has been designed ...'

Above left Rhododendron augustinii in the shelter of a windbreak, an early and essential adjunct to the garden. *Above right R. haematodes* with its rosy bells.

Three very different Scottish gardens

Left Logan Botanic Garden in Wigtonshire, with its 40 foot (12 metres) high cordyline palm trees, is in the south-west corner of Scotland, and basks in the warm breath of the Gulf Stream, to an even greater extent than the garden at Crarae, *opposite*. Opinions differ about the influence of the Gulf Stream. As the late Sir Herbert Maxwell, once wrote, 'No one wants to speak disrespectfully about it', but when you see the botanical treasures growing at Logan, plants such as the lobster claw (*Clianthus puniceus*), and the rare white form of *Lapageria rosea* one is forced to concede the blessings that the Gulf Stream can confer.

Above Kinross House in Kinross on the cool east coast, where Sir David and Lady Montgomery have a formal rose garden, enclosed in yew hedges. Its central axis leads the eye, through the haze, across Loch Leven to the castle in which Mary Queen of Scots was imprisoned in 1567. *Top left* Roses and spiral topiary at Kinross House. *Centre left* The architect was Sir William Bruce (d. 1710). *Right* Crarae Lodge, where Sir Ilay Campbell of Succoth and Lady Campbell have a west coast garden in mild Argyllshire. In it grow delicate rhododendrons and other plants, which enjoy the balmier airs of the west coast.

NORTHERN IRELAND

Precious plants at Mount Stewart

The mother of the present occupant of Mount Stewart, Lady Mairi Bury, who now runs the famous garden under the auspices of the National Trust, once wrote about her early days at Mount Stewart. 'The really exciting and important thing about Mount Stewart was discovering the climate and this, I think, I may claim to have done; making the gardens round the house was the second step. Until we lived here, I had only had the experience of gardens in the coldest parts of England, and the far north of Scotland. I had never visualized a garden with possibilities such as exist in Devon and Cornwall. I soon discovered that the climate was congenial to many half-hardy shrubs, and especially to the more tender Rhododendron species, acacias, which we call mimosa trees, and Banksian roses. Groves of eucalyptus trees, cordylines, palm trees and many kinds of bamboos add to the subtropical effect of these gardens, as well as the massive ilex trees and enormous tree heaths which give an Italian appearance to the scene.

'Mount Stewart is blessed by what gardeners call a favourable climate. The house faces almost due south, and is but a stone's throw away from the salt water of Lough Strangford, which is almost enclosed at its eastern end where the land runs due south. The eastern shore of the Ards is on the Irish sea, and Belfast Lough sweeps right round the northern shore far inland. So narrow is the space between the head of Strangford Lough and that of Belfast Lough that Mount Stewart, to all intents and purposes, experiences island conditions. The climate is subtropical, and the rate of growth is remarkable. I think this is due in great measure to the humidity of the atmosphere; in hot weather we always have extremely heavy dews at night. We do not have an excessive rainfall. Situated as we are on the east coast, we reap, so to speak, the best of both worlds, as we get all the sun of the east coast with its drier conditions, as compared with the excessive west-coast rainfall and less sun.'

Today, soon after the visitor has entered the gates of Mount Stewart gardens, he finds himself on a path lined with tall *Eucalyptus globulus*, the Tasmanian blue gum. These were grown from seeds brought back from South Africa by Theresa, Lady Londonderry, in 1894, and are now about 100 feet (30 metres) high. Others, planted along the walk in 1924, are nearly as tall. They produce a pungent scent in warm weather; eucalyptus oil is extracted from this species. On the east of the path are: *Crataegus oxyacantha* 'Maskei', *Lonicera maackii*, a shrubby honeysuckle from the Far East and *Aralia racemosa* from North America.

Several paths from the Fountain Walk lead off, to the right, into the 'Mairi Garden', called after Lady Mairi Bury when she was a child. To the south of this garden is a very large New Zealand cabbage tree (*Cordyline*

Opposite Below the southern front of the house, round a lily pond, different low hedges are an unusual and attractive feature.

Top In spring, bold groups of *Beschorneria yuccoides*, a delicate plant from Mexico, flower in the shelter of the house walls. *Centre left* Orange-flowered *Zauschneria californica* revels in the sharp drainage of a dry wall. *Centre right* Red hot pokers (*Kniphofia*) and purple hydrangeas make a striking colour contrast with the glaucous blue-green leaves of *Cedrus atlantica glauca*. *Bottom left* Delicate *Melianthus major* is a plant which is seldom seen in English gardens. Here it makes a jungly bower for a prehistoric monster in stone – one of the fanciful touches which occur in the Mount Stewart garden. *Bottom right Calceolaria integrifolia* shows its yellow flowers at the base of one of the ubiquitous palm trees. *Opposite* The Bloody Hand of Ulster. The story goes that two Scottish clans raced from Scotland to Ireland and that whoever touched Ireland first was to possess the land. The McDonnell ancestor of the Londonderry family, seeing he was losing the race, cut off his hand, threw it on the shore and claimed the land ... a dramatic incident in Irish history commemorated in the Shamrock garden at Mount Stewart, and recounted, almost thirty years ago, by the late Edith, Marchioness of Londonderry, who created the gardens as they are today. The bloody hand is planted in red dwarf begonias.

australis), the leaves of which are still used for papermaking in New Zealand.

One part of the garden is planted only with blue and white flowers such as a white fuchsia, white *Buddleia fallowiana* 'Alba' and the white Bourbon Rose 'Boule de Neige'. Among the specimen shrubs surrounding this area are: *Pittosporum eugenioides*, the Tarata from New Zealand; *Fuchsia excorticata*, with rough peeling bark, spring flowering and also from New Zealand; *Eucalyptus viminalis*, the ribbon gum

of Australia, where it is used for timber and pulp (a sweet liquid is extracted from the bark, much appreciated by koala bears); and *Pittosporum tobira* from China.

The immense size of the Irish yews at Mount Stewart surprises visitors. The original Irish yew was discovered at Florence Court in 1780, in Co. Fermanagh.

The large rectangular area below the south front was one of the first parts of the garden to be laid out by Lady Londonderry. When describing Mount Stewart in the *Journal* of the Royal Horticultural Society in December 1935, she wrote: 'This great clearance and the subsequent design of the present garden were made possible by the employment of twenty ex-servicemen after 1918. The huge Irish yews remain, also *Magnolia grandiflora* on the house, from early days. The ground was levelled in 1919 and the following year saw the garden taking its shape. Originally the South Garden, this area, 100 yards by 50 yards (91 by 45 metres), was remodelled by Lady Londonderry, who wrote that 'the general idea of the stonework was taken from the Villa Gamberaia, near Florence, and the Villa Farnese at Caprarola, and adapted to the site. The design at Mount Stewart was duplicated – an eastern parterre and a western one – with a wide lawn down the centre. All the stonework was done by local men. An old stonemason, Joe Girvan, a native of Grey Abbey, was a great craftsman and made all the walls throughout the garden.'

The beds are now given to herbaceous plants with some shrubs and roses, all for late summer effect. The whole area has recently been cleared and replanted, keeping to Lady Londonderry's colour schemes but including eight corner beds of roses. Two are planted with 'Dame Edith Helen' (raised and named after Lady Londonderry by Alex Dickson of Newtownards).

Near the house terrace are groups of *Beschorneria yuccoides* from Mexico, planted in 1922 (see page 169). On the terrace walls are many tender shrubs and climbers, amongst them *Punica granatum*, a pomegranate from south-west Asia, whose juice produces grenadine and the skin, tannin.

Reached from the raised walk at the far end of the Sunk Garden is the Shamrock Garden, originally started in 1924, when a yew hedge was planted outlining the shape of the shamrock.

That great garden expert, Graham Thomas, who compiled the guide to the garden from which these notes are gratefully taken, wrote in conclusion: 'The garden at Mount Stewart is a magnificent memorial to a remarkable woman, who lived and enjoyed life to the full. This garden on the grand scale could only have been created by someone with initiative, imagination and an intimate knowledge of other great gardens. Lady Londonderry's gardening diaries remain with us, and it is difficult to realize in these days the vast quantities of plants that annually arrived from nurseries, and later, from many of the most noted gardening enthusiasts in the British Isles, with whom exchanges were made. Many tender plants failed during the Second World War and in occasional very cold winters, but enough are left to make us realize the achievement in embellishing a fine garden design with rare plants.'

Above The main terrace, with its luxuriantly planted swagged vases of geraniums and silver-leaved *Cineraria maritima*, palm trees and eucalyptus, has a meridional air. *Opposite* In the 'Mairi' garden, a summer house is set around with plantings of white flowers – agapanthus, galtonias, with a carpet of velvety grey-leaved *Stachys lanata* in front.

ENGLAND

The best, and most varied gardens, whatever is said about the climate

The longest section in this book is given to the gardens of England. First, because this is a book produced in England – written by an Englishman (though actually I am Scottish) – but secondly, and perhaps more important, because it is generally conceded that England has the best gardens in the world. The reason for this is not difficult to find. Whatever anyone may say about our climate, it happens to be the best in the world for gardens. In a word, it is temperate. Though natives of other countries think that it practically never stops raining in England, they are wrong. Occasionally, though happily not often, we wish that it rained more, or at least, more regularly. Too much rain never harmed a garden seriously – too little, as in the dread year 1976, can bring devastation, killing 200-year-old, irreplaceable beech trees. Occasionally, too, we have a winter which causes casualties. Few ceanothus, for instance, in some parts of England, survived one recent killing winter. But many, after causing their owners serious anxiety, sprang up again from the roots, and flowered as they had never done before. To restrain my inherent British passion for talking about the weather, I will just repeat that our climate, despite the occasional vagary, is temperate, and to garden in a temperate climate presents great advantages.

Then there is the fact that, in England, there is, among high and low, a veritable passion for gardening. That bank manager, after leaving work and chafing, in a traffic jam, at the delay in reaching his destination, is not worrying because his wife will be wondering what kept him, or perhaps because he has a secret extramarital assignation, but because he wants to get home to dead-head his dahlias. And the belted Earl, dozing on the benches of the House of Lords, is not dreaming of how he is going to vote on some important amendment to the Forestry Bill, but more likely, of whether he can afford to heat both his greenhouses next winter. But, in England, to have a beautiful, or even famous garden, is not the perquisite of the rich and titled. Some of our most celebrated gardens are, in area, quite small and few of our large gardens are as grand as those on the Continent. We have nothing to compare, remotely, with Versailles or with the terraces and fountains of, say, Frascati (page 105), but we have a variety of gardens which is unique in the world. In what other country could you find, for instance 'natural' gardens such as those at Bodnant, Pylewell Park, or Lydney (page 6), or hundreds of gardens all over the country with perfectly devised herbaceous borders, those at Leeds Castle, for instance, which show the great gifts of the celebrated garden designer, the late Russell Page? Or that other form of gardening, which has been called the great contribution of England to the art forms of the world, the landscape garden, such as the lake at Stourhead, and the creations of Capability Brown scattered all over the country. These gardens, if gardens they can be called, have no rivals anywhere. Some are, admittedly, great historic gardens, planted when America was a geographical expression, but they are today in their maturity, transcendentally beautiful: and they are still copied, on a smaller

Opposite In Huntingdonshire there is a most fascinating and well-planned garden at Abbots Ripton. The garden, with its many different and imaginative features is the creation in the last forty years of Lord and Lady de Ramsey. Here, the arches of a rose-hung pergola are underplanted with a low hedge of weed-suppressing, silver-leaved plants. To the right, *Senecio greyii* covered with the cheerful yellow daisy flowers it shows in high summer.

scale, all over the world, more often in public parks, but sometimes in private gardens too.

Because gardening in England is a passion which pervades people in all walks of life, and has done for centuries, some of our most famous gardens are several hundred years old; others have been made in the last fifty years. A word which sums up the fascination of English gardens, is 'variety'. Fashions and taste change all the time; new ideas take their place beside recognized and well-loved features, such as lawns, which have been part of our 'blessed plots' for centuries.

A notable trend in the gardening world in Britain today is the fact that almost every garden of note – from the largest and most historic to the smallest of village plots – are, on occasion, open to the public. These openings, for which a modest entrance fee is charged, are in aid of various good causes, the most prestigious of which is the National Gardens Scheme, which yearly raises about £200,000 for charity.

Below Also at Abbots Ripton, where the English taste for Chinoiserie is perfectly illustrated. Ever since the eighteenth century fencing in the Chinese style, Oriental pavilions, even pagodas, have settled down in English gardens, and made themselves look quite at home. To the left, a bridge which might have been designed by Sir William Chambers 200 years ago, is ideally sited. It, and the fanciful little building nearby, are recent additions to the lakeside scene.

Parham Park – a famous old West Sussex garden, recently replanned

Some four years ago the Hon. Clive and Mrs Gibson decided to make changes in the garden at Parham Park, one of the most famous Elizabethan houses in England. Their aim was to make it more labour-saving, while retaining its character and atmosphere. Old walls, dating from the eighteenth century or earlier, and ancient clipped yews were, naturally, preserved, but areas of former kitchen garden and scattered flowerbeds were grassed over. Some borders were abolished, and

some retained, but planted in the modern way – that is, to give interest and colour for many months of the year – using shrubs as well as herbaceous flowers; the shrubs especially being chosen for their long-lasting leaf colour, as much as for their flowers. Decorative trellis, a little in the Tudor style, was added. The herb garden was replanted. At the entrance to the garden a knot-path, again in the Tudor style, was laid out. It was a great pleasure and thrill to me to be entrusted with this work.

Above Cherry blossom and a magnolia welcome the visitor.

As the visitors enter the pleasuregrounds of Parham Park, should the season be the spring, two beautiful mature trees put on a fine show of blossom to welcome them. A Japanese cherry, laden with flower, and a sweet-scented magnolia. Turning right, the path leads past the newly-made knot garden, its diamond pattern made up of young box bushes, and areas of grey and honey-coloured gravel. At the centre of each diamond is an Irish yew (*Taxus fastigiata*), a most useful tree for its gift of looking mature, while still quite young. A little further on, high gates give access to the old walled garden, now reorganized. A

spectacular vista opens up. The main border, now in its third year but already looking well established, is lavishly planted with weed-suppressing shrubs, such as *Senecio greyii*, *Phlomis fruticosa*, and *Ruta graveolens*, with its bluish leaves. *Pyrus salicifolia* and *Robinia pseudoacacia* 'Frisia' give height, as well as silver and gold leaf colour. Star performer in this new creation is *Lavatera olbia*, with pink mallow flowers for months on end. *Alchemilla mollis* and *Polygonum affine* provide an informal edging. High above the mixed colours is an old stone urn. In it is set, as such ornaments were in the early sixteenth century, a

Above The new knot garden, with its serrated wooden edging. *Opposite above* The supreme white rose 'Iceberg', with the antlered summer house beyond. *Below left and right* Kipling's poem about herbs, on its pedimented board, and differing foliage in the Olitory.

'plant' finial of wood, fast weathering to a soft silver. An unusual feature of these broad twin borders is the background of a high fence embowered in creepers, roses, clematis and *Solanum crispum*, the climbing potato, as well as a most striking plant, widely used at Parham for quick effect, the golden hop (*Humulus lupulus* aureus), one of the quickest and most decorative of climbers.

A special touch has been given to the decorative fence by contriving windows in its construction, to allow views through the woodwork of an old orchard with daffodils, before the border plants have grown tall enough to obscure the openings.

There are many other features in the garden to catch the visitor's eye. A 'blue' path, with double flower and shrub borders planted only with plants either with blue flowers, or – almost more important for lasting effect – leaves of a bluish tinge. Glaucous-leaved *Cupressus allumii*, conical in form, give a note of formality, and are set at regular intervals, as are eucalyptus, cut down every other year so that they assume a blue-grey bush-like habit. *Ruta graveolens* plays an important part here, as does *Hebe pageana*, one of the best of all edgings. And, of course, all the much loved azure-tinted flowers of the English garden: delphiniums, the herbaceous aconites, globe thistles (*echinops*), and an original touch, on the fence behind, the bluest roses to be found 'Violette' and the Teutonic 'Veilchenblau', and, of course, all kinds of blue and mauve clematis.

The white garden, with two white stone cherubs as *genii loci*, shows white tulips in spring, an edging of a non-invasive form of cerastium (the sometimes-to-be-dreaded Snow-in-Summer), *C. columnae*, white daisy-flowered anthemis, and *Cornus sibirica* behind, with its white variegated leaves all summer through.

Further on is the rose garden, with

Top left A stylized 'plant' in weathered wood in a carved stone vase, a device much used by the Tudors as being decorative and labour saving. *Top right* White tulips in early summer. *Centre left* An Oriental-looking arch, wreathed with very English roses. *Centre right* In the walled garden, a cloudy mass of gypsophila. *Bottom left* The golden hop, *Humulus lupulus* aureus, curtains the new fence. *Bottom right* 'Windows' left in the fence to give views of an orchard beyond.

many roses of the original planting still scenting the air, and an old stone summer house, lately embellished by the addition of unvarnished oak astragals, made on the estate (as were the various new fences). Over the door hangs a pair of antlers from a buck in the Parham Park – a real Elizabethan touch. The Park at Parham is not quite as other parks are, but resembles a Chase – an area of ancient oak trees and bracken, and the haunt of deer. These are 'quite tame', it has been written, 'they have been used to visitors for centuries.'

Another feature of the garden is the herb garden, enclosed in its original high yew hedges, with symmetrical beds planted with most of the herbs listed in Kipling's famous poem which begins 'Excellent herbs had our fathers of old – Excellent herbs to ease their pain'. The whole poem is written out in beautiful script on a white painted board in the Parham herb garden, and decorated with drawings taken from Gerard's *Herball* (1597), written a few years after the beautiful old house of Parham was built.

Above 'A spectacular vista opens up. The main border, now in its third year, but already well established, is lavishly planted with weed-suppressing shrubs.'

Hatfield in Hertfordshire, where the young Queen Elizabeth I was told that she was Queen of England

The story of the garden at Hatfield House (built in 1607–11) really begins when Queen Elizabeth I's Secretary of State, Robert Cecil, whose descendants still live at Hatfield, was given the property by James I. There was already an old house, most of which Robert Cecil demolished; where the young Elizabeth had spent an unhappy period of semi-imprisonment, during the reign of her unloving sister Bloody Mary, and it was at Hatfield that she received the news of Mary's death.

Robert Cecil soon set about creating a garden worthy of his new house, which was to be a veritable palace. The present Lady Salisbury gives us this glimpse of the grandeur of the garden in the early seventeenth century: 'From the courts and terraces about the house, steps, lined by painted and gilded lions, led to a parterre. There were espaliers on the sides, and here fountains played. The designer was a Frenchman, the celebrated Salomon de Caux. From here you had a prospect of the Great Water Parterre, also designed by de Caux, where a French visitor tells us you could "see a vast number of fish pass to and fro in the water, which is exceedingly clear".'

There were other delights and extravaganzas, and though we are concerned with the gardens as they are today, it is difficult not to mention a few. A marble fountain with a metal statue painted to look like copper, four 'mounts', fashionable conceits of the day, and an orchard for which the Queen of France sent over 500 trees – and her own gardeners to help plant them. The great John Tradescant (c.1570–1638) was sent abroad to collect new plants; his bills, but sadly, not his garden plans, still exist.

The splendour of Cecil's garden did not last long. His son was a keen gardener but, by the mid-eighteenth century, decay had set in, and the remains of the great garden were swept away by landscaping and 'improvement' carried out by successive Lords Salisbury culminating in a frantic refurbishment in honour of a visit from the young Queen Victoria.

Of the gardens today Lady Salisbury, a brilliant and knowledgeable gardener, writes: 'The great house that Robert Cecil built still stands, save for a few small details, much as he saw it in 1611, a

Above The east façade, with newly added steps, and seventeenth-century statues from Italy. Against the balustraded wall, espaliered pear trees which eventually will be cut to fill the triangular space allotted them. *Below* The octagonal fountain in the west parterre may be part of John Tradescant's original garden of 1609–11. *Opposite* The west parterre planted with such old favourite Elizabethan flowers as Lady's Mantle (*Alchemilla mollis*) and Lamb's Lug (*Stachys lanata*).

Jacobean Palace marvellously unchanged.

'Our aim has been and will be to restore as far as is possible an intimacy between the house and garden.'

One of the attractive features which the present Lord and Lady Salisbury have added to their rejuvenated garden is a 'Sweet Garden', planted with scented things for all seasons – winter sweet and honeysuckle, scented tulips and crocus, a chocolate-scented perennial cosmos, a rare scented mimulus (most mimulus have lost their scent in the last half century), magnolias, mahonia, philadelphus and lilacs, daphnes, pansies and violas, a crab apple with flowers smelling of violets, and, of course, roses and pinks – old-fashioned pinks and old-fashioned roses, some going back to the seventeenth century, and perhaps grown in the original garden – a romantic thought.

On the east side of the house, where de Caux made his great parterre, there is another impressive addition, a terrace which had to be reconstructed when a muniment room was built beneath it. The perron, balustrade and wall are new, and the statues are seventeenth-century Italian. They came originally from a villa near Como. The parterre below the steps is formed by twelve box-edged beds planted with roses, tree peonies, peonies, iris and tradescantias, called after the famous Tradescant who played such a part in the garden at Hatfield nearly 400 years ago.

Lady Salisbury's vision is that one day the house and garden at Hatfield 'may be as harmonious as a woman's face in the right hat ... planted with the fragrant homely plants which filled the gardens of the Tudors and Stuarts with sweetness and the hum of bees ... a place of fancies and conceits fulfilling the idea of the garden as a haven where both pleasure and peace are to be found.'

Top left Foxgloves and roses in a bed bordered with box. *Top right* Jacobean brickwork by the old steps in the 'sweet garden'. *Centre* The historic façade of the Great Hall, antedating the present house, makes a mellow background for Lady Salisbury's new garden planted with flowers, shrubs and herbs that might have found a place in a garden of the sixteenth century. *Bottom left* An originally designed garden seat, set among flowers. *Bottom right Angelica officinalis*, one example of the many old English plants in the garden at Hatfield. Its crystallized stems are used in the decoration of cakes.

Bear Ash in Berkshire – a modern garden, but in the old style

There has been an attractive garden at Bear Ash, near Twyford, for decades, but when the present occupants, Lord and Lady Remnant, moved in a few years ago, they wanted to make some changes – add a swimming-pool, for instance – and also to make the garden easier to maintain, to streamline it, in fact, while retaining its old character, for it had been the home of Lord Remnant's mother.

Herbaceous borders were turfed over, as were outlying flowerbeds, and planted thickly with daffodils. A lower lawn was allowed to grow into rough grass, with primroses and cowslips.

Some rose beds inevitably had to go, but one was kept and planted with shrub roses, which need so little care, underplanted with weed-proof perennial geraniums, such as 'Buxton's Blue'.

The most spectacular change was near the house, where an upper part of the old garden made way for the swimming-pool, and a brick retaining wall was embellished with an attractive willow-pattern fence. This is not only decorative, but it prevents children falling into the border below.

This border is a great feature of the 'new' garden, and has been planted in the modern manner; that is to say, not only with herbaceous material, but with low, ground-growing shrubs with coloured leaves, such as the admirable *Lonicera* 'Baggesen's Golden' (good-looking all year round), silver, weed-smothering senecio, red berberis, blue-leaved rue and the exotic-looking *Euphorbia wulfenii*.

Under the windows of the south-west facing façade, there was already an attractive terrace: here the beds under the walls were widened and planted with different greens, such as low junipers and bergenias. The pink house walls were already well-clothed with roses, and a bottle brush tree

Above A Chinoiserie fence tops a retaining wall, above the modern-style border planted with multicoloured shrubs and herbaceous flowers.

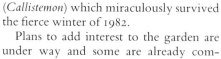

(*Callistemon*) which miraculously survived the fierce winter of 1982.

Plans to add interest to the garden are under way and some are already completed such as twin knot terraces of pink and grey gravel, a good example of a new fashion in English gardening. Part of the slate paving of the original garden has been gravelled, and the slates used to make the groundwork of a projected 'Silver Garden', of which part is already planted, with that excellent new ground-coverer, *Lamium maculatum* 'Beacon Silver', much in evidence. The adjoining 'Gold Garden' will be bright with yellow roses, golden elder, origanum and so on, all achieved with the help of an enthusiastic part-time gardener, John Hopwood, a talented artist, and not only with a spade.

The soil of the garden at Bear Ash is heavy clay, so roses, such as a newly-planted 'Aloha', do well, as does *Clematis* 'Barbara Dibley', that useful July-flowering clematis which is so shy of direct sunlight. The garden is, of course, filled with Lady Remnant's favourites such as the sweetly-scented *Mahonia japonica*, green flowered hellebores, and the elegant winter-flowering *Prunus subhirtella*.

Above The view from the drawing room window, over the flower-grown terrace. The stone 'toadstool' is a staddle stone, once used to stand barns on, as rats are supposed to be unable to climb them. *Below* One of the two new terraces of coloured gravel, in a diamond pattern and with a neat cushiony bush of hebe, as centrepiece. Part of the pattern is outlined in rope-edged Victorian tiles. *Opposite above* If given the position it likes, rich soil and a wall for support, there are few more showy roses than 'Aloha', a fairly new rose, raised in 1949, in the United States, by E. S. Boerner. *Below left* Clematis 'Barbara Dibley', above a carpet of silver *Stachys lanata*. *Centre* Old roses underplanted with dianthus, white helianthemum and silver foliage. *Right* Roses are happy in the clay soil of the garden, with their roots kept cool under the paving.

Ringfield in Kent – a garden of roses and long green vistas

Sir David and Lady Smithers moved in October 1944, to Ringfield, Knockholt, where Sir David was born in a house in the village. In spring 1962, they set about making a new rose garden. How successful they have been can be seen here.

The whole garden at Ringfield has an unfussy quality, which gives it grandeur without pomposity, and it has a sense of space, with wide vistas leading to interesting eye-catchers. The architect of the rose garden was Harold Whitelegg.

Favourite old roses are 'Mme Abel Chatenay', 'Frau Karl Druschki', 'Hugh Dickson', 'Mme Caroline Testout', 'François Juranville', 'Mme Alfred Carrière' and 'Zéphyrine Drouhin' – all classics. 'Pink Favourite' is a special success, as is 'Ena Harkness', still growing in the bed where she was originally planted; so are 'Peace', 'Mischief', 'Dame de Coeur',

Opposite The garden at Ringfield in July with bright 'Sarabande' roses on the terrace edge, and carefully clipped topiary on the lawn. *Above right* A statue acts as eye-catcher against a dark background of Irish yews, framed with high conifers. The flowerbeds are brightly set out with white-flowered grey-leaved anaphalis, and massed dahlias. *Below right* In the distance, a graceful bust surveys the scene from its marble pedestal, and a stone bench offers relaxation. *Above* The welcoming front door with a hanging basket of geraniums.

'Wendy Cussons' and 'Grandpa Dickson'. An acclaimed newcomer is 'Silver Jubilee', 'the best addition to the garden in fifteen years'.

On the bank surrounding the hedged rose garden, Sir David has planted sweetly-scented yellow 'Chinatown', which is pegged down – a treatment which makes for a brilliant display of flower over a long period.

Sir David is a founder member of the South of England Rose Group, of which he was President for three years. He gives them credit for steadily improving his system of spraying and feeding. This consists of foliar-feeding with Phostrogen, mulching with farmyard manure and three yearly applications of Vitax Q4. For spraying, Sir David relies on Nimrod and Benlate. 'The perfect rose,' he says, 'should blow, not only bloom, well. "Ernest Morse" that brilliant red, fades to an unpleasant purple. "Alec's Red" goes very grey and tatty round the edges; but the Hybrid Tea "Pania" dies like an aristocrat, as do "Peace" and "Peer Gynt".' Sir David admits to the peculiarity of disliking roses with split centres for cutting, and they are 'never allowed into the house', and Lady Smithers feels just as strongly about gardeners' dirty boots.

There are roses everywhere at Ringfield. Mixed borders near the house, and two round beds of 'John Waterer', 'the best of all reds'. More red roses are set where they can be seen from the kitchen window, and catch the evening light. One wall is curtained with 'Pink Perpetué'. Two other roses which specially take the eye are the little red 'National Trust', which lasts so well when cut; and 'Stephanie Diane', beautiful, though it needs regular spraying. There are a few bushes of a Smithers family rose, the 'Rev. F.Page Roberts', called after Sir David's grandfather, who was once correspondent of the Royal National Rose Society. It is yellow, but a weak 'doer', though 'the sweetest of all'. 'Even sweeter', says Sir David, 'than "President Herbert Hoover" after which I think they named a famous American statesman.'

Above left The formal rose garden, seen through an arch of yew. *Above right* A closer view of the bust shown on the previous page; the flowery, informal hedge in front of which it stands, is of long-flowering potentilla 'Elizabeth'. *Below* A view towards the house, again in a framework of tall conifers. In the foreground, a tub planted with cardinal red dahlia; 'Doris Day'.

Leeds Castle – a 20th-century garden for a 13th-century castle

Leeds Castle in Kent has often been described as the most beautiful castle in England, and with good cause, as its setting, in the middle of a lake, surrounded by parkland and centuries-old trees, must surely be unique. Remarkable women have played a part in its history, like the indiscreet Lady Badlesmere in the thirteenth century, who was sent to the Tower by Edward II in punishment for her rude reception of his wife, Queen Isabella, with whom, at that date, the King seems to have been on the best of terms (the 'she-wolf of France' apparently developed her lupine

qualities later). Centuries on, the rich, immensely generous and half American Lady Baillie, almost a Queen in her own right, bought and restored the castle, and filled it with art treasures. Before she died, she endowed the Leeds Castle Foundation as a centre of medical research and of the

Above Against a background of creeper and walls, a richly planted border of delphiniums and hardy geraniums – no better plants than these to smother weeds. *Right* The oldest parts of Leeds Castle date from 1119.

arts, with special emphasis on Anglo-American co-operation.

Recently, a new attraction has been added to complement the lake, the park, the vineyard (there is a record of a vineyard at Leeds in Domesday Book) and the castle itself: this is the new Culpeper Garden, called after the famous herbalist Nicholas Culpeper (1616–54), though it is not simply a herb garden. Nicholas was a relation of a seventeenth-century owner of the Castle, Lord Culpeper, whose son was Governor of Virginia in 1680–3. This new garden was laid out by the prestigious garden designer, the late Russell Page, on what he himself described as a 'shapeless but sunny plot', that was once a vegetable garden. It is framed on two sides by stables and cottages and old brick walls. The overall pattern is simple, to enable you to walk this way and that, through a field of blossom. The lush beds are planted with flowers which, though the average gardener thinks of them as English, have actually, over the centuries, come to our country from all over the world – including some, like the old-fashioned bergamot 'Cambridge Scarlet', from America (where it is known as Oswego Tea), that bountiful land with which the Leeds Castle Foundation has so many ties. The talented young head gardener, Stephen Crisp, mentioned some of his special favourites: *Aster amellus frikartii*, which is 'unlike most

Opposite above The great, and unhappily, late Russell Page's sure touch is much in evidence in the bold design of box-edged paths enclosing closely planted multi-coloured beds of flowers. *Below* Set in neat paving, near the entrance to the castle, is a sundial in a framework of old roses. *Right* Garden seats are judiciously placed round a terracotta pot planted with long-flowering daisy-flowered anthemis. *Below* A plant which is a star performer in the garden is the blue-flowered Jacob's ladder (*Polemonium*).

asters as it is self-supporting and not subject to mildew'; *Cosmos atrosanguineum*, maroon-crimson and chocolate-scented, which also originated in America; the seldom seen *Diascia rigescens* from South Africa, 'orchid-like pink flowers all summer long'; and *Rosa rubrifolia*, attractive in flower, foliage and fruit – 'What more could one want?'

The planners of the new borders at Leeds have specialized in effective plant combinations – the cerise, hardy geranium 'Russell Pritchard' growing under shrub roses, for example – and as every plant is clearly labelled, a visit to the Culpeper Garden is not only a pleasure, but instructive as well.

Old Toll House in Somerset – almost a cottage garden

Oak trees and a giant sycamore, 'guardians of both garden and house', shelter the garden, which until a few years ago, was Mrs Harrison's domain, from the south-west wind which prevails in her beautiful, but breezy corner of Somerset. The Old Toll House, near Yarlington, is set in a garden of three-quarters of an acre, and was created by Mrs Harrison. All she found were the things you expect to find in any neglected cottage garden: a few old apple and plum trees, some overgrown shrubs, and the usual matted grass, brambles, broken bottles and unidentified bits of iron. On the plus side, there were the protective *genii loci* – the sycamore and the oaks – a good *Cotoneaster cornubia*, a *Crataegus monogyna*, hedges and old walls, and, not to be overlooked, a coin of 1790.

Mrs Harrison aimed at making a garden with an atmosphere of serenity. 'A place where my friends and I could sit and relax and enjoy not only the sunshine, but the shade, too.' Asked about her garden philosophy, she replied with down-to-earth good sense, 'Concentrate on, and be thankful for, plants that thrive. Dismiss as nonsense anything about a labour-saving garden. Like children, plants need one's love and care; and who has ever heard of labour-saving children?'

The soil of the garden is heavy clay and so the accent in the garden is on roses, but not exclusively. Other favourites are Christmas roses ('coming into flower when they do, they seem miraculous'); daffodils, 'February Gold' and 'February Silver', for their early flowering, 'Pheasant

Above A petal-strewn path. *Opposite above* A rose-wreathed wall. *Below left* A gate and close-cropped hedge. *Below right* Close-set plants defeat weeds.

Eye' for its scent; peonies, especially 'Alice Harding' for its tint of amber. When asked which plants did well for her, Mrs Harrison replied, 'All bulbs – when not eaten by mice – philadelphus, delphiniums, viburnum – lots of things, really, ground elder included.'

In summer roses, of course, are the highlight: first and foremost, *R. rugosa* 'Belle Poitevine', vigorous enough to make a good hedge, and with recurrent flowers and spectacular hips; the rich red 'Josephine Bruce', English-raised, with dark-green foliage; and the transcendent 'Constance Spry' with its double pink flowers.

Rose-time sees the garden at the Toll House at its peak. That is the moment when cars in the lane stop and cameras click.

Below Climbing and rambling roses are a feature of the garden of the Old Toll House, and flourish in the rich clay of Somerset. Among the most successful that drape the trellised walls, and festoon old apple trees, are the bridal white 'Wedding Day', child of *R. sinowilsonii*, and the buff yellow 'Emily Gray', which likes to be planted in a sheltered place, and about which the Royal Horticultural Society's *Dictionary of Gardening* issues a warning, as being 'reported in the United States as not reliably hardy north of Maryland'. A third is the dashing and vigorous, deep purple-crimson 'Commandant Beaurepaire'.

Mottisfont Abbey in Hampshire – a flower-filled garden by the River Test

Mottisfont Abbey, near Romsey, dates back to the last quarter of the twelfth century, and was once an Augustinian priory. At the time of the dissolution of the monasteries, in the reign of Henry VIII, it became the property of Lord Sandys, the King's Lord Chamberlain: the house was largely rebuilt years ago. The grounds of Mottisfont are bordered by the river Test, and the garden is famous for the collection of old roses assembled there in the last nine years by the National Trust. It was planned and laid out under the direction of that best known of rosarians, Graham Thomas. The Abbey itself was given to the National Trust in 1957 by Mrs Gilbert Russell, and the old kitchen garden, with its warm brick walls, offers the ideal site for a rose garden.

In his introductory notes to the booklet about the garden, Graham Thomas tells us: 'The garden is the result of several years' work in preparing the ground and assembling a very special collection of roses. Provision has been made for some 300 varieties and the garden is not yet com-plete. Many are the renowned varieties depicted by Pierre-Joseph Redouté for the Empress Josephine, who started, by her extensive collection at Malmaison, what has grown into the modern craze for roses. Together they form a group of plants with a colouring, style and fragrance that has never been surpassed.'

These are some of the roses at Mottis-font which catch the visitor's eye: 'Alister Stella Gray' (a man or a woman?), which has flowers of gold, and will quickly grow to 15 feet (4.5 metres) in the shelter of a wall (its buttonhole buds are yolk-yellow); the fascinating 'Baron Girod de L'Ain', a vigorous Hybrid Perpetual shrub rose with deep crimson-purple flowers, of which the petals are uniquely piped with white; 'Paul Neyron', another Hybrid Perpetual with luscious peony-sized flowers; 'Mrs John Laing', an English-raised rose, with large cup-shaped, mauve-flushed flowers, which are excellent for cutting; 'Empress Josephine', which now for some reason has been given the clumsy name of 'Francofurtana', with silver pink flowers, which always seems to be the loveliest of all the gallicas; and 'Cerise Bouquet', a modern shrub rose, with sprays of bril-liant, crinkled flowers.

And last, that much-loved of old roses, raised in Luxembourg at the time of the Crimean War, 'Tour de Malakoff', which that matchless describer of roses, Nancy Lindsay, called 'an illustrious shrub with emerald foliage and cabbages of magnolia purple, shot *gorge de pigeon*'.

These are just a few of the 'old' shrub roses in the garden at Mottisfont. But Mottisfont is not a garden for one season only. Though many of the roses there flower but once in the summer – a weak-ness, it must be admitted in many species roses – there is much else to see in the garden from May until October, the herbaceous borders are as good as any in England.

Above Mottisfont Abbey, once an Augustinian priory.

197

Above left No herbaceous flowers give more colour for a longer period than achilleas, such as 'Golden Plate'. *Above right* On a hot summer's day, the box hedges smell with a delicious pungency. *Left* Foxgloves seed themselves about every year. *Below* A brimming border with a quartet of closely clipped conifers to break the skyline. *Opposite above* A cushion of that excellent German-raised rose, 'Raubritter', overlaps the central pool of the walled garden. On either side, Victorian scissor-back seats. *Below* Informally edged twin borders benefit from the shelter of the wall.

Luton Hoo in Hertfordshire has a famous rose garden, once the scene of a Royal romance

On 2 December 1891, Luton Hoo, a large, comfortable house in Bedfordshire, was the scene of a distinguished romance. At a house-party, while the other guests were dancing in the ballroom, a pale young man with a seductive moustache proposed to a quiet, serious-looking girl with golden hair. The scene was the boudoir of their hostess, Madame de Falbe. 'Of course I said yes,' wrote Princess Mary in her diary. The young man was to be the future King of England, and charming: but Princess Mary's first romance was short-lived, and Prince Eddy, Duke of Clarence, died the following year. The Princess sensibly married his brother, afterwards King George v.

It was one of the first of the future Queen Mary's many visits to Luton Hoo, the last being in 1950, when, as an old lady, she inspected the famous collection of Fabergé objects which the house now holds, and walked round the celebrated rose garden.

The story of Luton Hoo begins many, many years ago, when the land belonged to the de Hoo family. Hoo itself is a Saxon word meaning the spur of a hill, and is often met with in East Anglia. In 1762 it was sold to the unpopular Prime Minister of George III, John Stuart, Earl of Bute, shortly before his resignation.

Lord Bute was more popular with the gardening fraternity than with his fellow politicians and the country generally, an unpopularity engendered by his reactionary political views and the equivocal position he filled in the Household of the Princess of Wales. But he was a great botanist and lavish patron of horticulture, and he can be credited with having used his influence with Augusta of Saxe-Gotha to encourage the foundation of Kew Gardens. Such was his fame in the world of horticulture that Linnaeus named stewartia, a beautiful plant of the Theaceae family (which includes camellias) after him. Though he spelled the plant's name wrong, as the Bute family name is Stuart.

In 1773, when Dr Johnson visited Luton Hoo, it was finished, and Johnson was, for him, full of praise. 'This is one of the places,' he conceded, 'I do not regret having come to see.'

Sir Julius Wernher and his wife, Lady Zia, grandparents of the present owner Mr Nicholas Phillips, bought Luton Hoo in 1903. The gardens were laid out by Romaine Walker in the fashionable style of the day. Capability Brown's park had originally swept right up under the windows of the house, but this was not to the Edwardian taste, so a terrace was added, above a balustraded lower terrace edged with borders of flowers, which in late summer are sensational. Measured steps, in graceful circular form, led down to the rose garden, which is now one of the great rose gardens of England, and the most beautiful roses reward with months of flower the attention and care lavished on them by Lady Zia's grandson. Lady Zia herself had a rose named after her – an accolade for anyone who loves roses. As a great gardener, the genial Dean Reynolds Hole, wrote many years ago, 'He who would have roses in his garden, must have roses in his heart.'

Left A gate with graceful vases of carved stone leads to a topiary arch, with centuries-old cedars beyond. *Opposite* A luxuriant wisteria drapes a wall and another vase of pearly stone. To the right, *Weigela* 'Eva Rathke', covered with its deep red, pale-eyed flowers.

Above The Rose Garden, with its yew hedges and classical temple. In the foreground, a sundial 'only tells of sunny hours' and the end of a herbaceous border. The corner plant, popular for its architectural effect, is *Bergenia cordifolia*. *Left* Herbaceous plants spill over a gravel path. *Right* Ferns and low growing shrubs in the Rock Garden.

Town gardens

Anyone who has ever made a garden in London, or in any other large town, will tell you that success or failure depends on faithfully following a few established rules, which have been proved over and over again to be reliable guide-lines.

On taking over a new town garden, it is essential to check the soil and the drainage. Best of all, but expensive (with best top spit loam at a small fortune a cubic yard, plus labour), is to renew the top-soil of your garden completely. Peat helps to conserve moisture, and regular watering is all important: it is no good relying on rain, however, much we complain of the climate. All town gardeners stress the value of bone meal as a fertilizer; it is effective and clean to handle. One rueful town gardener once told me: 'I imported 180 sacks of earth from the country, a back-breaking job which I hoped would result in terraces like the hanging gardens of Babylon, but all it did was disappear.' It is better, and certainly far cheaper, to make the most of the earth you find; but you must dig it, enrich it, lace it with peat, and water it constantly. A garden water tap and a hose are absolutely essential. For roof gardens, efficient shelter from wind by glass or wattle screening is important.

Magnolias, and the invaluable golden-leaved *Robinia pseudoacacia* 'Frisia', all do well in town conditions. The knowledgeable advise against laburnums, as little will grow under them. You should choose

Above The Hon. John Stuart's Chelsea garden, seen from an upstairs window. A bold pattern of box hedges, white lilies and 'Iceberg' roses. Garden designer, Vernon Russell advised on the plan. *Left* The garden of Mr and Mrs John Cates in Mayfair with white impatiens, trellis and Chinoiserie metal furniture.

shrubs with smooth, shiny foliage which sheds town dirt easily. Camellias do well, and some really dedicated gardeners sponge the leaves of their camellias which makes them look 'rudely healthy'.

Other shrubs which are proven successes are veronicas, buddleias – if only to attract butterflies (and one remembers how well they thrive in London, when colonies of them took over bombed sites in the City) – syringas, hibiscus, golden euonymus, and choisyas with their pungently spicy leaves; hollies should be avoided, as they tend to poison the ground around them. For groundcover, periwinkle, hypericum, bergenia, all the lamiums (though *L. Galeobdolon* is apt to take over), and the ever-useful *Cotoneaster horizontalis*.

As for flowers, roses are never really

successful, and seem to flower for a few weeks only, an exception to the rule being the ever-to-be-relied-upon 'Iceberg', as can be seen in the picture opposite. Hostas give of their best, and can be interplanted, for more colour, with annual plants. If the garden is on the shady side then the town gardener's best friend is impatiens, the much loved Busy Lizzie, preferably white. Tellima and *Euphorbia robbiae* will also put up with almost complete shade.

With a little ingenuity, small gardens can be made to look larger. Mirrors can be used strategically, and vistas created by trelliswork. White, or colour-washed walls will lighten the scene, always important in a large city. An eye-catcher, such as a statue or bird bath, will give interest and discreet floodlighting flatters the simplest town garden.

Above left and right The historic Chelsea Physic garden, founded in 1673, offers better growing conditions than most town gardens. By the pond, a luxuriant *Phormium tenax*. Bordering the wall of Swan Walk, the oldest *Kohlreuteria paniculata* in England. *Below left and right* Good-looking furniture, and crisp trelliswork are valuable assets in any town garden. To the left is Mrs Thomasina Beck's garden in Stockwell. To the right is Mr Leslie Dawson's in Chelsea.

The American Museum near Bath

Claverton Manor, in Avon, is the first American Museum to be made outside the United States. It was founded twenty years ago by Dallas Pratt and the late John Judkyn, 'an American and an Englishman with a deep appreciation of the American arts and a desire to increase Anglo-American understanding'. It has been enjoyed by hundreds of thousands of visitors ever since.

Claverton Manor itself is a grey Bath stone building designed by Sir Jeffry Wyatville, the architect of King George IV, for whom he transformed Windsor Castle. It was built in 1820.

The Museum is set in romantic countryside, richly wooded, and looks over the spreading valley of the river Avon. The park and beautifully laid-out gardens provide an ideal setting for such outdoor exhibits of unusual garden decorations as a Conestoga (a kind of covered wagon) and an Indian teepee. One part of the large gardens is modelled as a replica of George Washington's rose and flower garden at Mount Vernon, Virginia.

In its twenty years of existence, the American Museum has attempted, most successfully, to interpret the history and arts of the United States. Its talented and imaginative director is Ian McCallum, a Scotsman who knows and loves America.

Opposite above left A pair of eagles survey the view over the Avon valley. *Above right* A vase full of flowers. *Below* The milliner's shop, with its baroque windows. *Above* The garden modelled on George Washington's at Mount Vernon. *Right* A dipping pool in a grottoed alcove. The large-leaved plant is *Rodgersia podophylla*.

ACKNOWLEDGEMENTS

Most of the photographs in this book were taken by the author. Exceptions are:
Patrick Matthews, p. 10, above left; Mr J. Drayton-Hastie, pp. 14, 15; Japanese
Tourist Board, pp. 32, 33, 36; Jean Claude Lamontagne, p. 38 top three; James
Mortimer, pp. 46, 47; Andrew Powell, pp. 49, 50, 51, 52; Natalia Keffer, p. 53;
Gerti Deutsch, pp. 93, 94; Roustan, pp. 122, 123, 124; Countess Oeynhausen,
p. 147 below left; Earl of Dartmouth, pp. 148, 150, 151; Mr V. Kennett, p. 149;
David Paton, p. 165.

The following people and organisations have been helpful in providing
illustrations: the Japanese Tourist Board pp. 32, 33, 36; M. de Montpellier
d'Annevoie, pp. 126, 127; The Netherlands Board of Tourism, p. 137; the Swedish
National Tourist Office pp. 156, 157.